See Man Jump...
See God Fall

By

Joey Bond

PROMOTION
PUBLISHING

See Man Jump...See God Fall

©Copyright 1997

by Joey Bond

Published by:
ProMotion Publishing
3368-F Governor Drive, Suite 144
San Diego, CA 92122
1-800-231-1776

ISBN: 1-57901-001-6

Foreword

Is there on Earth a fullness of joy, or is there no such thing? Is there some way to make life fully worth living, or is this impossible? If there is such a way, how do you go about finding it? What should you try to do? What should you seek to avoid? What should be the goal in which your activity comes to rest? What should you accept? What should you refuse to accept? What should you love? What should you hate?

What the world values is money, reputation, long life, achievement. What it counts as joy is health and comfort of the body, good food, fine clothes, beautiful things to look at, pleasant music to listen to.

What it condemns is lack of money, a low social rank, a reputation for being no good, and an early death.

What it considers misfortune is bodily discomfort and labor, no chance to get one's fill of good food, not having good clothes to wear, having no way to amuse or delight the eye, no pleasant music to listen to.

If people find that they are deprived of these things, they go into a panic or fall into despair. They are so concerned for their life that their anxiety makes life unbearable, even when they have the things they think they want. Their very concern for pursuit of enjoyment makes them unhappy.

The rich make life intolerable, driving themselves in order to get more and more money which they cannot use. In so doing they become alienated from themselves, and exhausted in their own service as though they were slaves of others.

The ambitious run day and night in pursuit of honors, constantly in anguish about the success of their plans, dreading the miscalculation that may wreck everything. Thus they are alienated from themselves, exhausting their real life in service of the shadow created by their own insatiable hope.

What bitterness! Man's thirst for survival in the future makes him incapable of living in the present. He lives for what is always out of reach!

Those who are caught up in the machinery of power take no joy except in activity and change - the whirring of the machine! Whenever the occasion for action presents itself, they are compelled to act; they cannot help themselves. They are inexorably moved, like the machine of which they are a part. Prisoners in the world of objects, they have no choice but to submit to the demands of matter! They are pressed down and crushed by external forces, fashion, the market, events and public opinion.

Never in a whole lifetime do they recover their right mind! What a pity!

Chuang Tzu - circa 400 b.c.

---

* Excerpted quotes of Chuang Tzu, translated by Thomas Merton, from *The Way Of Chuang Tzu*. Copyright © 1965 by The Abbey of Gethsemani. Reprinted by permission of New Directions Publishing Corp.

TABLE OF CONTENTS

See Man Jump...See God Fall

To - Bubby & Zedy

INTRODUCTION

We are caught on a swirling vapor in an untamed void, seemingly forbidden to descend and touch the common ground of our own beginnings. We are the inexperienced voyagers falling into the bottomless sea of time, locked into an evolutionary plan for renewed transformation.

The reptilian hisses of antediluvian antiquity can still be heard in our whispers although we have abandoned the ancient roads and portentous pathways that assert our unity with life. It appears that we are destined to know the dark beyond the stars before we comprehend the nature of our own souls.

Our human wanderings, that are captured in the steps of the primitive warrior and then again in the mental calculations of the nuclear scientist, are attended by the storms and darkness of surging dreams and compulsions which hover over our greatest achievements.

My attempt is to create a rift in time where life will vault backwards to encounter itself upon its evolutionary road. The lessons within this text are dedicated toward learning how to live an uncontrived life, and one that is devoted to the day at hand.

It pursues a course for the refinement of the senses and involves a study of the importance of conscious and intelligent control of the coordinated physical functions of the body and the mental aspect of our being, all of which is emphasized throughout the greater part of this book.

Years of personal study and private investigation uphold the provision of a teaching and practice that is many hundreds of years old and my central aim is to provoke discussion.

Tranquillity is the crying need of our age, but what it is and how to attain it are still compelling questions. One must learn to recognize the opposing forces and to deal with them in the stride of life, and this book explains ways of thinking about the impasses, difficulties, and dilemmas through introducing new methods in dealing with the convolutions of daily living.

Further still, I have chosen to open the magical window of imagination that gleams between the forest and the city, and this stream of thoughtful light will help the reader recognize the diversity of self-protective guises that are odiously fastened to human behavior and the need for affection across the illusions of form.

New and fierce rays of nuclear light issue from the thin white cities and the world machine of technology ticks like a remorseless clock in the dead and confined air of our assembled scientific priesthood. Wrapped in the thick fog of our own puerile fascination with inert matter and novelty, all appears as a wild uncertainty, and we are left on the merry-go-round of social machinations while reality always eludes our grasp.

To know ourselves, to penetrate the mystery of the soul, is the voyage that stands as a monument of both Man's homelessness and his power, and within the great sea of self-reflection, we wait for the upwelling of that inner tide which will finally engulf the ancient traveler.

The crude cleverness of technology drives the heartbeat of our time-conscious generation, therefore let us wade into the sea of infinite reflection which is haunted by that single tear that falls so gracefully down a child's face.

For those who visualize an end to the trivial and magicless dimension of the social masquerade and to those who wish to wander in the finer colors of reality, may this book serve as passage on a great ship on the long journey home.

—Joey Bond

"When Greek mythology's Prometheus, above, gave man craft skills and fire, a wrathful Zeus chained him to a mountaintop, then punished mankind by releasing Pandora's box of evil. The myth reflects traditional societies' uneasiness with progress."

Heaven-Storming

"Force maketh nature more violent in return"

— Francis Bacon

Like a big red ball, the sun slowly rose into the bleached and acrid sky. Somewhere below, in the early dawn of his ignorance, one lone creature squats with the back of his hairy hands pressed into the earth.

He stares stupidly upward, rubbing the cold night from his naked body. What little he grasps of the world around him comes in great part from his imagination, and from what he manages to draw from his simple-minded elders. He shuffles along, his steps a shambling but springy run, an awkward bouncing along all fours. In one hand he is clutching a crude hunting-weapon and with the other he uses the knuckles of his closed fist to propel himself forward.

He is an animal, like those he hunts and is set upon a ceaseless search for prey. He will forage untiringly along a well-worn trail that leads him daily to the kind of sustenance that will satisfy his omnivorous appetite, and to a struggle in what is after all, a desperate battle for survival. He looks back, swiftly turning his grisly head and peers into the jungle bush, then thinks of how far away he is from the dismal cave-dwelling he calls home. He apes along, continuing upon a sloping path that steers to a higher observation point, and from there he will have a much needed advantage in his fearful battle for existence.

The hunter-animal is equipped with stereoscopic vision and from below a dense ridge of furry brow his sunken eyes glare menacingly from within the cavernous idiocy of his thick skull. He cautiously relinquishes his grip on the handle of his incult weapon and places it down. He angles his armored cranium downward toward the hard cold earth. He is bemused at the unfamiliar tracks laid down in the stone-cold mud, then stabs one hairy finger into a thin and shallow slit.

The tiny ditch he scrapes at has been hardened for perhaps millions of years and the creature has no way of knowing that the concreted prints belong to a leather-winged bird that etched its claw-markings in what was once soft silt.

The ape-like animal cannot even begin to imagine that he is peering into a distant past that holds the writings of a story once belonging to a mighty bird long since departed, having vanished on the winds of time.

Suddenly a sound breaks loose in the brush behind him; his body tenses, he gathers all his attention, and listens. He reclaims his weapon and scrambles over to a nearby tree; his upper lip curled backwards. He interprets a menacing sound and abruptly tears upward, like any other frightened animal, and disappears in the upper branches. Somewhere above, the sound of the dying crackle of twigs and branches reveals a sense of failure that has fallen over the creature.

Some two million years ago, Pithecanthropus, the erect man-ape, straightened his back and angled his lurid head toward the black dome of the sky. He searched among the pinpoints of flaming lights and his fascination with the fiery beams infused him with a wondrous desire to duplicate their radiant mystery; to somehow reach closer to their brilliant energy. Haltingly he rose, pulling himself upward, and in his new-found balance discovered novel sights, sounds and smells which enlivened his quest for survival.

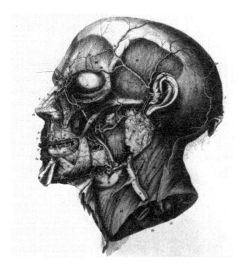

"The erect man-ape angled his lurid head and searched among the pinpoints of flaming lights."

Like a child, he discovered a new power; he rose to his feet, however ineptly, and he **balanced.** His freed forelimbs, now lightened of their load, reached outward and upward. His eyes skillfully adjusted to the greater variety of sustenance; to proteins and sugars, now available to him at this new height, and his diversified diet would go on to influence his temperament, his undertakings, and his reason for being.

Movement would take on a whole new meaning, for he would now establish a distinct relationship with "running quadrupeds;" some of which he would devour and some that he would wisely domesticate.

With his head floating in the sky and the soles of his feet pressed into the earth below, he found himself standing, and the far-reaching savanna lay open to his attack. His "higher" frame of awareness secured his evolution. The trees belonged to him and sitting atop their outstretched limbs he viewed the world through a 'larger window of perception.'

Indeed, his ability to **observe** became the value of his life! This creature, would become Man; with fleshier legs, manifesting thicker lips, his teeth less protrusive, and the forehead appearing considerably higher. His history is told from the animals he ravaged and from their bones, hides and parts - from them he constructed his weapons and donned a wardrobe of clothed comfort which would protect him and his family from the dangers and inclemencies of primitive life.

With his low skull-vault he gathered his articles for survival and with a meager assortment of wood-chips and stones, and through an intensified group cooperation, he endured the earth's hot summers and drifted through the chillbreath of winter.

A familiar story, yet why did we **concoct** this saga?

We must keep in mind that the faces of our earliest ancestors remain forever unknown to us and whatever truth we seek resides in the same gray anonymity in which primal man's most formidable enemy, the saber-toothed tiger, and along with it the dinosaur, is lost. Nevertheless, offered for your perusal is a version, an anthropological curiosity, which is one of a misportrayed adenoidal cretin with the proverbial club in his hand.

The puzzle of human evolution peaks our curiosity, but there is something more to the story besides rummaging through skull and bones!

In the world of fossils and prehistoric remains do we not truly seek the soul of man himself?

Thus we are forced to depict it from the vacuous eye-sockets of incomplete skulls and from the partiality of artists hurried to implant their own conceptions, whether sculptured or drawn, upon the insensible dead. Yet if we 'dig' a little deeper into our ancestral past we will discover that what has been left out of this stereotypical rendition is a social creature known to have buried his dead with little gifts and selected offerings, and ostensibly attended the injured and disfigured among his kind.

Has modern man changed his mind-set from this early myth? Have we reached beyond our fears, our doubts, our thirst for domination, or the desire for power?

Even in the modern world, do we still not struggle for comfort and safety? And yet there *is* a more gentle place where we are led by childlike emotions and propelled by the invisible art of our dreams!

Within the creature called man exist the figures and patterns of an uncertain future that will be created from his own essence.

Are you searching for a deeper inspiration that will draw an atmosphere of truth to your inner-sense of reality? Perhaps you are searching for the substance of your existence; for the unfeigned meaning of your life!

The pathway of life is a journey amidst strange and magical obstacles that is taken every day; it is an inward journey that shapes the mind and molds feelings. It is here within the matrix of the mind that the human being wanders, sometimes aimlessly, yet ceaselessly amongst the fantastic fragments of thought, amongst the haunted debris of broken dreams, and through the pristine palaces of future plans.

"...the urban heap of existence atop the skulking materialism of the thin white cities."

Some of us, adrift in dreamy ignorance, can only sleepwalk through the dark storehouse of unconscious life. Still, in dreams, there are those of us who walk across a jeweled rainbow and some who ride the comets of space where falling stars burn briefly, holding promise for all their hidden wishes. We all live with the great desire to reach deep into the beauty and mystery of our cherished dreams and hope to concretize our splendored fantasies, envisioning ourselves standing in the brightness of our own inspiration. Whoever we are, the genetic dice have been thrown against the intangible walls of the future, and the events of mankind are left to the chance of urban dreams; the urban heap of existence with millions of human beings stacked one upon the other.

On the face of the earth the victims survive, as it were, working so oppressively and so long, that the air of day is hardly breathed and the light of day is rarely seen. Here they are robbed of aesthetic, intellectual and spiritual substance. Within the walls of meager satisfaction they sit embezzled of their intrinsic energy, and the disposable masses sit menacingly on the brink of emotional inflammability.

For now, what 'is-to-be' will be found in the skulking materialism of the thin white cities, and in the end we appear to be shaped by the mutability of fortune and favor.

There is an invisible journey that you are on, a journey where once immortal navigators trod, seeking an enchanted reality. It is an ancient road that leads to a discarded past; an abandoned route adrift in mystery and superstition.

This is an epic journey that speaks to us of tremendous achievement, wonder and terror. It is the story of man, his suffering, his lurking paradoxes, and his progressive alienation from the universe.

Yet through this great adventure, which is at once filled with menace and meaning, with hope and loneliness, we can still see the face of **home-yearning** man. He has seen his future through the imaginings of a poet, and he has viewed his past through the eyes of a desolate child in Hiroshima. He searches for the way to his heart and his habits have grown in such a way as to be denied it. He seeks a place that will nurture his soul. He dreams of a time when he will be free to choose his own direction.

Yes, man dreams! He dreams with eyes closed and he dreams with eyes open! Did man envision that two million years ago the rock he held as a clumsy tool would be replaced by a scalpel? Did he imagine that the crystal and ruby stones in his cave-dwelling would be harnessed in such a way as to generate the power to measure time, or bring back sight?

"Could prehistoric man have imagined that 'ruby-stones,' imbedded in his cave-walls, would be harnessed to bring back sight?"

Indeed, Man's reality is found in his capacity to dream! One monumental dream that all men have is the need for knowing their destiny and the purpose of their life. It is a desire for self-comprehension; for a freeing coolness that will grant psychological equanimity and emotional groundedness. And then again, there is an anticipation to see humanity arrive at the gentle crossing of world peace and unite as a great family of trust. Yes, with each vision there can be found great discovery and man has unearthed the reality of just how much he craves peace.

"The dreams of Mankind have propelled him toward remarkable discoveries."

We are left to wander through the smoke of dreams searching for another doorway that will perchance lead to a new dimension in experience. The quest draws us to an entrance that reveals a self-authenticity; one that moves beyond the experimental sounds of triumph and disaster, beyond winning and losing. We will find ourselves drifting freely along a heightened plateau where we can experience an inspired moment of self-reality, and our awareness will take flight. It is a metaphysical passage, an upward soaring on a current of transformation, supported by the wings of imagination, and sustained by the breath of faith. Yet, if the quest is limited to mere thinking, the search would be but a shallow moving of prospects. If confined to bare hope, the journey would remain a sunless expectation, a whimsical sleep without self-comprehension and therefore without blooming. Even if our meditation be attended with resolve, we will only repeatedly suffer a circuitous journey through the limited senses of a finite awareness, and the dream will have no other power, in the end, than a vicarious supplication, and indeed will be relegated to a drawn-out deception. It is curious that both the dreams we seek and the nightmares we fear are projected from within!

Still, it is all that we have, these dreams of ours, and throughout recorded history the dreams of Mankind have propelled him toward remarkable discoveries, as seen in his expeditions into the farther reaches of space, and as evidenced by the curious excursions that have taken him into the vast expanse of the ocean deep, and then again to hidden territories found in the earth itself. These combined regions encompass our knowledge of life, as we know it. However, there is yet another frontier that lies much closer to our observations and whose borderlands remain a profound mystery. It is the sphere of the most puzzling creature that has yet been encountered in this universe: it is the domain of the paradoxical entity known as the human being!

What are we searching for when we depart for the outer limits of the cosmos? What do we seek at the bottom of the ocean floor? It is in actuality a gesture, a striving to solve the riddle of life and the meaning and purpose of human evolution. This cryptic predicament has led the 'mind-explorer' into exacting mental and physical disciplines in the endeavor to fathom the mystery of creation and perhaps discover the role that humankind plays in the scheme of life. Through the cultivation of philosophy, science and medicine, metaphysics and religion, Man's attempt to integrate himself with the so called *inner-way* has been an exercise in the meaning of 'self'; if such a self truly exists!

Let's prepare our bags for our excursion into less familiar territory and allow me to be your guide on this journey which will take us along a new corridor of experience, beyond the rising city-flurry of hypnotic redundancy that covers our real identities; away from the empirical sounds that define the past in terms of technical success, and on to a euphony that connotes a less categorical tomorrow.

We will set out for the Orient, taking with us our Western rationality; anchored as it is in technology and empiricism, and we shall venture onto metaphysical and numinous terrain that is somewhat steeped in primitive superstition and then again radiantly colored by visions of mystical illumination.

Let us step lightly and abandon ourselves to the sublime enchantment of ancient artifacts and to exalted intuitions that have been left behind by the preciseness of scientific explication. We will make our passage into timeless regions and once again will come upon forgotten 'revelations' that have been muted by the soundless flight of passing time.

The way lies in a winding expedition that is thick with the red dust of ancestral acts that perchance will rise again behind our vague steps. Let us then turn and allow ourselves to descry a wisdom-treasure that belongs to an ancient and cherished practice that is one of the noblest teachings that human genius has brought forth.

In our sojourn we will make our way to the land of 'Tai Chi Ch'uan'! We must steady ourselves so as to venture to higher ground and perhaps enter the domain of the *'grand and ultimate,'* which is the literal translation of *Tai Chi*.

This ancient road leads to fertile fields of flowering awareness and from the intellective branches we may have cause to yank on the apple of wisdom. What we will bite into shall be half ratiocinations arrived at by science and the other half will taste of ambrosial conclusions via the wondrous reality of self-illumination. And perhaps we will come to see that the 'sweet and sour' of our visit are as complimentary halves of the same great fruit of self-awareness.

Let us walk along the ontological and hidden trails that have prepared man for the future and draw heartily from the well of knowledge that keeps us connected to the adventure of life, and more reverently to a sophic past, that is after all, from whence we gained our understanding of Man.

What little we know of our true beginnings shall suffice for our stay, as we look at the philosophical underpinnings of a well-worn book of knowledge and step into the mind-garden of China's great treasure that exists in service to the health and welfare of the human spirit.

The Orient has made noteworthy contributions in charting this 'hidden realm' in hope of finding the fugitive specimen called 'self.' Penetrating the inner boundaries of this elusive entity has been the work-zone of an ancient healing-art system that comes to us from old China and is known as 'Tai Chi Ch'uan' (pronounced as 'tie jee chew-en').

Through the practice and study of its components, tenets and gleanings, we have been left with a design, a platform, as it were, for self-comprehension. The lessons have been handed down through a mnemonic pathway and partly through idiographic script.

"Tai Chi has been handed down through a mnemonic pathway and partly through ideographic script."

Through this composed and aesthetically charming system we are given an invaluable opportunity to gather our scattered thoughts and center our energy, so that we may penetrate the inner boundaries of the human mind, and further gather and harvest the organic energies of the human body. From this higher plateau of self-composure we may then reenter the world with balance and a new perspective.

"The Chinese originated the 'magnetic needle compass' which every boyscout and mountaineer is familiar with."

Tai Chi is a window onto the inner world of 'being' where one can hear the note of self-reality and the ethereal echo of one's true voice. Here within the gentle fields of the 'inner playground' we have the making of a journey to an inward-directed sphere of activity which reaches beyond the limits of our mechanical thinking and transcends our ego-based responses.

It is here within this sanctuary of self-awareness that we are granted the opportunity to heal the body and reveal the mind!

Let us look through the multifaceted windows of an Oriental jewel that has not been tarnished by time nor circumstance. The map we will study has been charted by the gifted minds of a great ancestry; one that was concerned with direction, both material and spiritual, inclusive of the outward and inward.

As examples of the ingenious methods of approach when encountering 'space,' as it were in the outer, temporal world, the Chinese devised not one, but two styles of compasses. This race of people invented the traveler's 'magnetic-needle-compass,' which every boy scout is familiar with, and which every mountaineer is dependent upon.

As well, there is the lesser known invention, but most brilliantly composed 'south-pointing chariot,' whereupon no matter which way the chariot is made to be pointed, the hand-crafted charioteer, (sitting atop the chariot), is caused to pivot around, and ultimately face in the opposed southern direction. While tarrying on the subject of direction, there is also the sextant, this being another Chinese marvel which guided ships by way of the stars.

As much as these inventions are profoundly impressive, they point more clearly to the wealth of awareness possessed by the Chinese civilization and to those rare individuals who came to create these gems that have impacted our whole way of relating to space and time. Further still, these inventions demonstrate how art and science did indeed merge in mellifluous synchrony.

While on the subject of invention let us take a small detour and ponder the creation of the first mass-produced **bronze-coin**, which is an inceptive crafting by the Chinese called 'cash,' meaning ready-money. There is also the creation of our paper-money that comes from **pulp-paper** which also happens to be a Chinese innovation.

We have been privileged to enter into countless cultures, as well as to share the views of the greatest thinkers and planners through the remarkable fabrication of paper that has permutated into a form that is taken for granted; it is an invention that you are holding in your hands right now; it is the bound book, which the Chinese created.

Further still, the protraction of this singular work, as evolved in the hands of the Chinese, became early on, the indispensable 'encyclopedia.'

In fact the largest book in the world can be found in the Chinese department of the British Museum Library which contains a single work that occupies no fewer than 5,020 volumes. This wonderful production of the Chinese press is one of only a small number of copies now in existence. It is an encyclopedia of the literature of China, covering a period of twenty-eight centuries—from 1100 b.c. to 1700 A.D.

The work owes its literary proclivities to Emperor Kang-he, who reigned from 1662 until 1772. His undertaking was great when he appointed a commission of learned men to have the original documentation reproduced, seeing, as he did, that the contemporary works were extensively corrupted and such errors had been allowed to creep into modern editions. This work took forty years to complete and Kang-he died before ever seeing it realized.

On a more general note, the "encyclopedia", continues to be a splendid entry into every child's education and may well be viewed as a *gift* from the Chinese to humanity.

Have we all not reached up with eager fascination to that high shelf and pulled away a prize of untold value in its reading; passages that took us to a world of marvel and to lands that, without ever so much as a single step, let us wander through the jungles of Africa, and to euphoric worlds of impossible dimensions beyond the stars.

Yes, through the window of the 'book' and its organized complexity, we have shaped the mind and given life to the psychic and emotional tone of young and old alike.

It was Aldous Huxley who said, "Every man who knows how to read has it in his power to magnify himself, to multiply the ways in which he exists, to make his life full, significant and interesting."

Bountiful in artistic insight, wise in scholarship, and representative of monumental builders of civilization, the Chinese managed to make the difficult breakthrough from art to science, indeed melding art and science. They have given the world a treasure-trove of potent 'tools' and meaningful 'directions.'

As much as the Chinese were intrigued with the conditions of space, they were equally fascinated with the movement of time which was captured by the invention of the first mechanical clock created by Yi Xing and Liang Lingzan in 725 a.d. Fascination with the progress of things gave rise to this extraordinary contrivance which set the stage for a new order in man's relationship to universal operations.

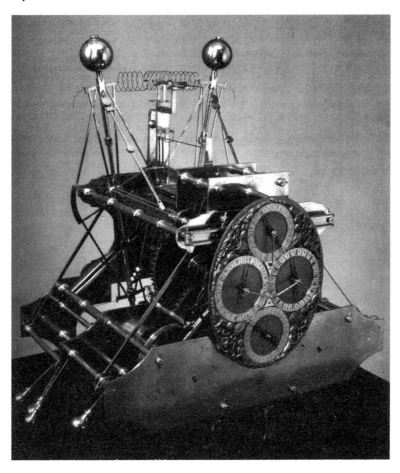

"The Chinese invented the first mechanical clock, created by Yi Xing and Liang Lingzan."

Within the labyrinthine world of its turning wheels and delicately coiled wires, small adjustments were needed to maintain its ordering, and this microcosm of mechanical organization would go on to become a symbol of 'control;' a mechanism which would sardonically end up ordering the gamut of human activities.

Indeed, the symbol of our artificial civilization is the clock. The alarm sounds and we resist its hollow call by pushing against its numbered face for another five minutes of hallowed darkness.

In terms of the human organism itself, mechanical time is an interloper. While social life has its own routines, the throb of the pulse, the inhaling and exhaling of the lungs, also change from hour to hour with strain and activity. We are, each of us, controlled by an internal time-clock, known as our 'circadian' rhythm which determines when we will awaken, when we will sleep, and is connected to the cycles of energy related to our physical and mental states.

Unquestionably, civilization gained in matters of efficiency by the installment of the clock, but at the expense of an incremental standardization that turned Western man into an automated piece of his own handiwork. This was the signal of the encroachment of technology into his way of life.

Time is demonstrated not so much by the calendar but by the affairs that fill it.

As 'time' went on in its relentless march, the lives of the vast populace were commanded by quite a different pacemaker. Later, as witnessed in the English industrial population of 1870, cities were fueled by the movement of commerce, by supply and demand, and at the heart of operations stood the accuracy of time-keeping which 'punched-in-and-out' with mechanical exactitude.

The pendulum swung freely and deliberately, and the way in which man began thinking swung in an altogether new direction, as time became a consequence of his labor.

What was becoming altogether more evident was the necessity for him to conform to the mandates of a technological culture. Indeed, time and its manipulation would 'wind' its way into the fabric of every social activity; its 'little hands' reaching even into the private darkness of our emotional content.

Emotional trials and psychological difficulties are linked to its ticking calculations when we say, "Time heals all wounds!"

In a deeper sense, perhaps related to man's search for longevity, and then again his thirst to discover an answer as to his place in the greater scheme of things, time symbolized not only terrestrial, but even cosmic correspondence. In the rhythm of his calculated imprisonment, the control of time was in a sense a delirious conquest over man's failure to comprehend the clockwork of the universe.

Now, social change is no longer the largest issue, but rather constant and sightless transitions that have no purpose. There is an array of arguments against permitting the continuation of present scientific-technological trends in our society. The question that begs modern man is whether it is achievable to draw upon the winnings of scientific and technological advancement and yet avert the devastation of our natural environment or the depravation of the dignity of human life.

Can we not manage the orientation of technological inventiveness and ensure that the heirs of tomorrow will have a future by focusing on the individual person and his environment?

These are concerns that will affect our future as a race, and while we focus on these issues, there are other significant considerations as well, ranging from the poisoning of our water systems and therefore the food we eat, to the wasteful depletion of our natural resources, as we cut down forests and groves, and 'ore' away, while killing our Great Lakes, which all ties into the extinction of entire species of plants and animals. Further still these operations lead us to feelings of insecurity and hopelessness.

All are part of our rapid social change, with its concrete, tar, asphalt, steel and glass, and sonic booms splitting the air at 120 decibels disturbing millions of people's sleep violently.

In ascension are eugenic programs purporting to beneficially manipulate the quality of our DNA and alter the human race, while leaving behind the impoverished spirits who fill the ghettos.

We need to think deeply on the fate of mankind which is pursuing a carefully designed course in recklessness.

Yes, grand wizards of the future, we have arrived at the gates of the Information Age; a domain that is replete with brilliant devices that are **intended** to lighten the load of labor and quell uncertainty.

After all is said and done, indeed, man has become an infected little unit in the equation of progress and mass communication, and as his numbers grow so does his insensitivity concerning his fellow man, his individuality and his destiny.

We are left to take the last exit, to turn and take a 'detour from reality' and observe the transmission of the 'old-world science' into the 'technology-of-the-new.'

Let us therefore contemplate the future and honor these cultural artisans of the 'old east' who have made their contributions, trying as they have to set an enlightened course for humanity.

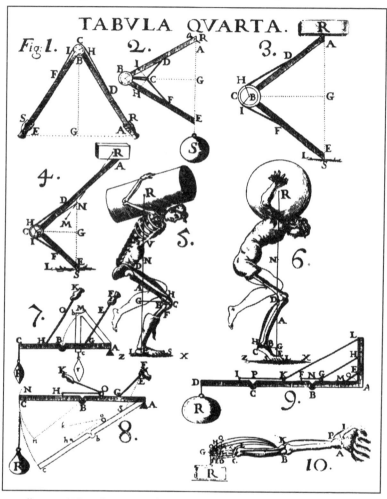

"...to lift the weighted atlas of confusion and penetrate the unfinished future."

Let us also keep in mind that not all inventions and discoveries are material or mechanical in nature and the most intriguing belong purely to the mind and its inventive power. The passageway has been set by those rare and ancient thinkers whose secret wanderings have come through the time-zone of the psyche; those special few who have cultivated the soil of ontology and turned the earth of philosophy.

The way has been cleared by those who have polished the antique mirror of longevity; those cherished individuals who have reached into the wondrous pool of resplendent health, having shown us that well-being is ultimately reflected through embracing both body and mind. They are the ones who have given us the power to comprehend the past, and with their gifts of material and spiritual substance, we are better able to cross the bridge of the 'wanting-present' and penetrate the unfinished future.

It has been by way of their offering, through understanding the mind of man, his behavior and tendencies, that we are more capable of forging our way into the expanse of self-awareness and into the aesthetic realms of creative-being that mold our future with renewed originality.

In this field of operations, related to higher consciousness, we will look at the relationship between subject and object, experimenter and experience; a quest which has forced scientists, metaphysicians, mystics and pragmatists to abandon the ordinary world of experience and to move, perhaps somewhat unsteadily, toward the unknown regions that lie beyond the narrow margin of sensory perception.

Indeed, in the three hundred years of scientific method, we have discovered that there are drastic restrictions imposed on our sensory equipment, and we have come to see that when considering the range of sight and sound given to man, there are punishing limitations placed on his experiential potential. As we have come to understand, through the great advancement of science, where vision terminates and hearing ceases, there still vibrates an unimaginable and phantasmic world which we uncover only through the investigations of our assembled scientific apparatus. Because of these inherently stifling impingements and having been faced with the weakness of man's capacity to express the 'inner-quality' of his being, 'explorers of new realities' have rallied and instigated a search for further dimensions in experience which will help one and all reach 'higher ground.'

They, for now remaining nameless, have nevertheless pushed unremittingly toward the most subtle concept of spontaneous and flowing 'self-expression'; an expression that will free the mind to wander into limitless reflection and to pass through to an authentic soaring beyond the finite scope of inherited and second-hand thinking.

The philosophical and metaphysical under-pinnings under consideration, which come under the name of Tai Chi, is not a bringing forth of doctrines. Nor is it merely some intellectual picture of the world. Neither is it a dogmatic skepticism, but actually represents a new attitude which pulls on the inner thread of self-comprehension.

The mind-body voyager and the free thinker are united in their purpose and begin an evolution where they become inter-linked to the very substance of existence and merge into the deeper fabric of self-reality. This is often perceived as a 'forbidden journey' and one that departs from 'normal' life. Although it is a precarious thread it nonetheless connects the individual to the whole of living, and those who seek the truth of self-reality will dare to walk this numinous strand that is so terribly close to snapping.

Indeed, this map christened Tai Chi, can be seen as a medium for infinite reflection and for achieving a degree of contemplation which can become conscious of *being*. It points to a level of awareness that moves beyond the lopsided obsession with 'self-image' in the egocentric sense, which is after all, empty of essence.

Aside from the inherent limitations placed on the human sensorium, life in the modern realm of social activity has become, more and more, a marginal experience, and has become proscribed to the narrow events that confine man to the chores of everyday existence; a substantiality which has caused the disquieted individual to retreat from so-called *reality*. Furthermore, the social workings of the 'mechanical jungle' have made it necessary for those who may be called 'pioneers of the idiopathic' to walk along a rather critical line separating scientific method from metaphysical approach.

One pressing question that surfaces consistently is whether we may hope to arrive at a measure of ease that will seed the future generations with a safe and peaceful environment? It is all the more clear that gentle pastimes have undergone considerable development. Aggressive preoccupations and activity have become greater and have become popularized in proportion to social refinement. Today, we have ample opportunity to release our negativism through a variety of sordid affairs.

Some pastimes at their very basis, foretell the future of man's continued taste for violence and direct the ultimate demeanor of so many a child.

We have only to examine a typical fairground which at first may appear as an elaborate playground. Tucked away in one of its many corners is however another reality found in one of its clamorous arcades, that being the 'shooting-gallery.' In this darkened corridor lies a festival for militaristic and murderous behavior. For a couple of quarters every child has the opportunity to hold a gun, or rifle in their hands and to shoot at wooden ducks and birds, or mow down clapboard flowers. And in more ample establishments, children come face to face with thoughtfully costumed mannequins who have been made to walk and gesticulate through an ingenious mechanism. Here, little boys and girls can gun down some figurine, who may be seen walking, or running along, while some puppets appear alone, and still others in groups. There are a few placed in decorative settings, with monkeys climbing up ropes, while some figures can be seen tumbling out of windows and popping up out of trapdoors.

These varied figurines and dolls and puppets, altogether, seem to almost be real, with arms and legs moving, beaks snapping, wings beating, some dressed in rags like a destitute person, others dressed in satin and gold like celebrated royalty. The entire group of animals and humans in readiness for slaughter!

After just a few firing rounds there grows an odd feeling that these characters may indeed possess intelligence, perhaps a soul, that they may be alive!

You can almost hear them calling out: "Don't kill me!" "Have pity!" And in the excitement of the clamor and racket, if the child keeps one eye shut (to the crime of killing) and the other carefully aimed at a beak, or a head, they will hardly have time to notice an odd sensation that rises like a rush of warm blood in their mouths, and they will continue in their unbridled play with a fierce intention, accompanied by delirious outbursts.

They most certainly find great amusement as the animals collapse and the figures smash stupidly about, and all without insinuation of anything bloody to them. And there in the din and bedlam and metallic clamor they will carry out their assaults devoid of any suggestion of assassination. To watch as the parent eggs the child on to "aim well," and with exhortative verbal proddings bid their child to; "Shoot at the heart!," or; "Get him in the leg!," and again to; "Knock his head off!" these pleas add to the horror of what now amounts to manslaughter.

Yes the cardboard animals and mannequins and wooden puppets are no longer bits of lifeless carvings, for the children have worked themselves to a frenzy, to a point of emotional exhilaration and disturbance where all these forms are endowed with veins and brains, with life and blood!

Here in this innocent game of 'bump-off,' lies the evolution of a distinct attitude in behavior that sets the stage for attenuating physical violence by giving it a legalized outlet which is further supported later down the road through military occupations, industry, law, and the more obvious pastimes found in sports like boxing, fencing, bull fighting.

So it goes, everything in reality only a reversion to ancient barbarity where man was on the same plane as the wild animals he chased. Is it so difficult to see how modern day hunting is less than a slightly altered pursuit of earlier protocol?

Indeed, the 'hunt' is after all, a rather thin coating of rationality for the atrocity found on so called protected reserves that have been sardonically set aside for 'culling' the herd. In the same vein of

"The legalized custom of slaughtering innocent animals siphons off our bloodthirsty resentments."

behavior there follows the pigeon shoot, the killing of pheasant and quail, and just about anything that moves.

The opportunity we have created through these legalized customs is to siphon off our destructive energies and blood-thirsty resentments. With blind wantonness there proceeds the slaughtering of faultless deer with rifle fire, decapitating bears, blasting rhinoceros and elephants, and killing innocent game birds in meadows, and surely without these vents our brutal presentiments would no doubt be turned on ourselves.

Murder is broadened to the rank of duty and prevails to the point of heroism. There are religions that extol the ferocity of their multi-armed gods who gorge themselves with human lives and those who are encouraged to adore the slaughter of the infidels who would dare believe in any other god.

The disdain of human life is inculcated from infancy and given free reign in the legalized slaughter of war, where men, women and children whom we do not know, let alone hate, are mowed down like wheat fields and all in the regulated, regimented, and obligatory name of national security.

Here is the naked face of brutal murder that is saddled with the red of human blood and where individuals are rewarded with oxymoronic medals and honors for their bravery in destroying human life. The merits by which the individual rises above others, and the virtues which win him honor, celebrity and fortune, are based entirely upon aggression and fed by the murderous mania of destruction.

That these subnormal tendencies can be ascribed to the environment of daily influences, or cultural, political and religious intervention, may in some small measure be arguable, and we can certainly add the bloody passions of instinctual behavior based on ancestral survival in the wild. To turn this dirtied coin over, we can also see that the diversified violations upon human beings are nonetheless accompanied by belated qualms of conscience, remorse, and are resolved in episodes of devotion, friendship, affections, refinements of civilization and sociability.

Through this curious and deeply disturbing dichotomy we arrive at the muddy stream of human existence that proceeds in its formidable manipulations, sinister struggles and odious transactions, that at once embraces the stench of corruption and yet cultivates the presence of purity, poetic mood, silence and moral rehabilitation.

These are the preoccupations of a world that at one end strikes the bell of existence with technological inventiveness and the other end with the savage vestiges of atavism. Crushed as we are by these multiple and piercing ruptures which speak of interminable sufferings and danger, and yet ardently supported by the gentle souls who carry the torch of joy, pity and love, we face the future on the human ship of evolution.

When we look back along the path of early times, Man's only possessions were an undeveloped mind, simple weapons, and an exposed body dressed sparsely in animal skins, and this was all that protected the individual from an overwhelming and predominantly hostile environment. This instinctual creature has fought his way to the elaborate and sophisticated guises of modern times and survives today because he is still a man - and Man has created his own universe.

Through the turbulent and violent eras of earliest human existence and into the sophisticated terror of the twentieth century, nature implores man to demonstrate his native intelligence and remove himself from the depleted and confined air of his laboratories that descend upon natural events like noxious insects. Nature cries to Mankind that he may do away with the fierce and desperate rhythms that trample the flesh of the earth, the lives of innocent creatures, and the soul of his fellow man.

He has certainly scarred the land with his ceaseless investigations and bold experiments, and with his metal machines that plunder and tear. His life has been spent filling his atmosphere with roaring fumes, sulphury steam and hideous accidents.

Where once the stars danced in the milky magic of the blue canopy of space, now the skies are filled with the invisible fires of industrial poisons and speeding ships of information.

Rather than face the terror of the modern city and his ultimate responsibility toward the emotional environment of his fellow citizen, man finds escape through elaborate and costly rituals that find him plunging into space, leaving behind a threatening trail of atomic dust. Witness the path of our radical wanderings that have regurgitated vast quantities of enormous radiating machinery that spin uselessly in the space above. The further he travels from home the further he removes himself from seeing the desperate imbalance left in the modern world.

This is the great scientist, the three hundred year old experimenter in scientific method, who has blackened the stardust with his satellite launchings and blotted out the sun with his looming buildings. He has pierced the clouds with his sky-scraping towers and his waking and sleeping is choked with the endless noise of movement.

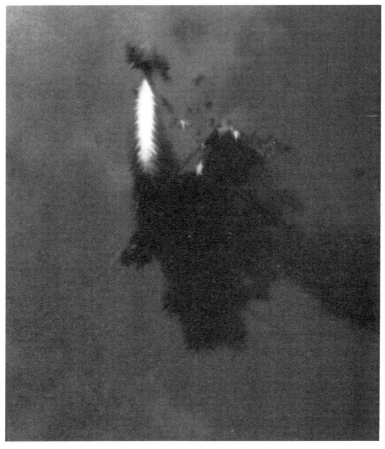

"Man's life has been spent filling his atmosphere with industrial poisons and hideous accidents."

Where once he sighed the crystal air, he now breathes in the smog and fog of his smoke-belching transportations.

Our cities which supposedly exist to create and nurture civilization present an entirely different aspect. And after all, where has this knowledge taken us?

Will our history be blown about on some plutonium-ridden field with our great edifices strewn and scattered about like a child's building set and our bones reduced to briquettes of charcoal?

How far can knowledge go without awareness of self?

"Will our history be blown about on some plutonium-ridden field and our bones reduced to briquettes of charcoal?"

When will we see that we must ready the body to examine the mind and that we need to clear the mind to see the self! Will we succeed in finding a method which will render our journey intelligible and free from the naked hostilities that stand in the way of establishing an attitude of peaceful contribution to the progeny of this ocean-planet? What will become of this place called Earth at the rate of our polluting the atmosphere?

What will become of humankind in so much as we are gravitationally pinned to a failing planet which is revolving through space at a speed of 68,000 mph?

So the story goes in every lesson taught to modern man, and one that reminds us, somewhat harshly, of an uncomfortable reality that points to ineluctable habits of fear and aggression.

We view man speeding along the uncertain terrain of the ever-changing future. His numbers crowd and push into the concrete and glass cities and he has spawned his way into the remote and shadowless canopies of our shrinking, far-off jungles.

In these places do we find homeless man searching for some resting place that will satisfy his hunger for freedom from the alarming conditions of a world that is out of step with natural order.

Life the timeless, mysterious gift!

Where are we going and what do we hope to find? What great gifts lie in store for us in the foreseeable future and what terrors wait ahead? Where is this strange and wondrous journey leading us and what will we discover? Do we still have time to design a plan which will cause the human race to become more profoundly sensible, free from hostility and prejudice, and escape from Man's unbridled desire for power?

Of all the gifts given to humankind, perhaps the most precious is his mind, and with this great and enigmatic instrument he untiringly struggles to uncover his purpose for being here amongst the shining stars and speeding satellites, waiting for the answer to the mystery of his existence.

We know what has happened, but we can never be sure of what is to come. There is no guarantee for success, nor could there be such assurance for **finite** human beings. And so, to vault our insecurities, we have placed huge emphasis on science and technology, and the questions that are raised follow thusly: What has been the value of scientific discoveries in biology, physics, or in space research in relation to man's capacity to live in harmony with his fellow man and stay in balance with his environment? Does technology serve him, or has he become a slave to technological devices that appear endless?

The evolution of scientific knowledge, as well as the scientific improvement of standing technology, has been remarkably the fruit of Western European civilization. The word technology was the creation of one Professor Jacob Bigelow of Harvard, who brought the word forward in 1829 in his essay entitled **Elements of Technology.**

Technology and its influence on human development and social progress reaches back as far as the middle ages with the perfecting of the process for manufacturing inexpensive steel, and then onto the invention of the incandescent filament-lamp produced by Joseph Swan in England in 1878, and through to Edison's stunning work with the creation of the phonograph, and most certainly includes Bell's astounding invention of the telephone, with continuing importance placed on the invention of the transistor, which made its momentous debut in 1947. Through these prime examples we can clearly see the transformational effects of technological innovation on social development.

But with the forward thrust of scientific knowledge and our magnified technological powers, which at one time pointed to a spectacular future for mankind, and which evolved to supposedly serve society, we are witnessing the antithesis of specialization. This paradox is apparent when viewing the deftness of automated work processes which has inadvertently robbed us of human satisfaction in personal accomplishments. Technological innovativeness is an adventurism that is largely responsible for undermining our job status, and is responsible for creating massive unemployment.

The framework of the physical environment of tomorrow may be drawn with very little distortion when considering the widening power of today's technological possibilities.

At the same time what needs to be carefully considered is that technological innovation has grown in its determinative strength as it wields its artful whip, bringing vast social changes, which has occurred during the past three centuries, in Western European civilization and to those cultures percolating from it.

It is difficult to admit that 'technology' has become the single largest factor in determining our future as a race when compared to political, economic, religious and intellectual issues. Although boosted by our technological paraphernalia, man's dream of mastering all aspects of nature takes no account of the real barriers of his circumscribed awareness. An obvious quandary that attacks our sensibilities, and a massive ecological tumor which technology has failed to cure, revolves around the various conditions of our material environment.

We can presume that the mistreatment and ensuing spoliation of nature is not an ephemeral problem but, by all means, has profound emotional and psychological roots.

If we look upon nature as intrusive to the aims and designs of humankind, we will most likely attempt to manipulate and override the forces of nature, heedless of the damage wreaked upon the environment. On the other hand, if we regard the vistas and offerings of nature as nurturing and beneficent, we would be hard pressed to ruin its beauty for near-sighted, temporal profit and more likely attempt to work within the scope of nature's circle of reference. However, the sound of freedom has become a sour note when we study our impudent attempts to commandeer natural forces and our striving continues to remain outside of **natural** cycles.

Then there is the theological problem of viewing man as the center of the universe and his domination over all of nature's activities; from chemicalizing natural fields of wheat and oat, herbiciding trees bearing oranges and apples, netting fish to abolition and slaughtering whales to their virtual extinction, while in general enslaving and crushing the will of blameless animals and even his fellow man.

While man mostly takes advantage of animals, for his survival, he is himself after all, a 'parasite' on the vegetable kingdom and must exploit nature in order to persevere.

The nature of our preferred disposition has been acutely conditioned by beliefs concerning nature and destiny, which is fastened to our conditioning by theology.

In bare terms; Christian pedagogy instilled the idea that God assembled the Earth for man's enjoyment and convenience.

This passage taken from the Bible in the opening chapter of Genesis points to a mental climate that is purely anthropocentric:

> *God created . . . the Earth . . .*
> *Let [man] have dominion over the fish. . .*
> *over the fowl . . . over every living thing . . .*
> *over all the earth;*
> *And behold; it was very good.*

So it was, by religious decree, that many propagators exploited nature without consideration of the long term effects. The image of steady and unconstrained progress, proposed by the religious fundamentalists, abandoned regard of the natural environment because the Judeo-Christian tradition had already made it subordinate to man and simply the object of his exploitative ventures.

But as history would go on to show there grew a new attitude related to man's need to commune with nature's pristine ordering.

During the middle ages, many localities had identified and successfully fought a 'scientifically capable enemy,' in the figure of rapacious mining corporations, who released the ecological-cover of Pandora's box and sent their industrial minions to tear away at metallic ore, and in turn wrought the devastation of fertile agricultural areas and furthered the destruction of precious forests.

So as to return to our train of thought, these outraged locals had political mechanisms put in place and made significant strides which prevented, in some small measure, the merciless corporate assaults on the environment.

To complete our eco-theological journey we need little assurance when noting that the natural environment can hardly withstand **our** technological assault, and we can peruse a foreboding statement taken from the **Tao Teh Ching,** (pronounced Dow Day Jing). This work represents the basic text of Taoist thought, dated circa 500 b.c and appears as a slim volume of some 5000 words classically translated as 'The Way and its Power,' or if you will, "The Ordering Principle Behind All Life." Study the divergent (and predictive) Chinese attitude toward man's relationship to nature expressed thusly;

> **Those who would take over the Earth**
> **And shape it to their will**
> **Never, I notice, succeed.**

Equally critical is man's advancing alienation from nature and his withdrawal into a technologically oriented culture. Where once man lay his weary head on nature's plenteous bosom, he now suckles on the rigid, plastic teats of technology. We are only beginning to see that there is a technological bond as well as an aesthetic one between man and nature.

Nevertheless, we assume that with enough time and expenditure of energy we will route the highways of space and weave the fibers of genetic strands to the image of our liking. Yet our thrusts into these unknown frontiers are limited by the number of trained minds that can shoulder these far-reaching expeditions.

Further still are the mounting concerns of the convoluted social problems that this research has imposed upon a naive society; a society that is waking to the reality that solutions to problems create problems.

Indeed, we are coming to learn that when we so blindly place our fate in the hands of scientific devices, which have been grafted to the appetites of commercial interest, additional problems mount exponentially.

"We watch man's advancing alienation from nature and his withdrawal into a technological culture."

Despite the advances, we are not any closer to conquering the regions of human interest that hunger for world peace, social order and personal well-being. We have not quashed corruption or violence - we have not eliminated the monstrous weapons of war and have in fact proceeded boldly to perfect them.

"We have not eliminated the monstrous weapons of war and have in fact proceeded boldly to perfect them."

The human race is not truly great by the asset of its arms, it is great by its *use* of science, and above all by its arts. And let us always keep in mind that the cogent correctness of science points only to a small part of the truth.

The purpose of existence cannot depend on the invention of a new materialistic dialectic led by our assembled scientific priesthood.

The main philosophical hazard to our freedom lies in the blind forces of technology which are collectively suffocating our capacity to determine our creative and political goals. The scientific estate must be infused with social purpose if we are to connect truly with the idea of progress.

The real question is how do we step beyond the calculated cleverness of technology which has failed to unite us as complete human beings and has simply tied us together as intellectual entities?

If we look at our advanced spacecraft we can better see how they exemplify in microcosm the status of man vis-a-vis the technological milieu in which he abides. These vessels are the most intricate and precise machines ever designed and assembled. Spacecraft generate their own electricity; they transmit television signals over enormous distances; they send some hundred billion bits of information back to Earth daily, as the ship navigates by way of celestial bodies with great precision.

Notwithstanding the craft's remarkable velocity, its speed and position can be detected with formidable exactitude at a distance of three hundred thousand miles. Yet the ship is not equipped with an equitable toilet, and potable water is drastically chlorinated making it offensive to drink, and astronauts are required to sleep in their seats. Finally, food is delivered from a freeze-dried, vacuum-packaged, plastic bag.

The disparity between the mechanical and cybernetic components that support the vessel and the lack of sophistication for sustaining life aboard is acute.

In application we can see that the increasing prepotency of the technological instrumentality of modern society is becoming notably incongruous with the culture in which technology performs.

Life, in a personal sense, is a 'becoming' from the world-within and the efforts made in the fragile search for self-reality should not stand second in line to our spacecraft and telescopes that impotently pursue the breaking-away of galaxies.

"The soaring to the stars beyond is pointless, unless it harmonizes with an imperative 'inward' expansion."

Let attention be called to the educators of this revolutionary 'Information-Age' and hope that they may adroitly conclude that the discoveries drawn from the labor of those whose aims are set beyond the orbit of Neptune, need emerge in at least equal importance with the transformations we may engender in the 'inner-laboratory' of self-awareness. The soaring to the stars beyond is pointless, unless it harmonizes with an imperative 'inward' expansion.

Within the framework of his artificial power and technological excellence, social order remains absent and human compassion wanting. Despite his incongruent attitude and his inability to stay in stride with 'natural order,' social-man has somehow managed to evolve.

While his communities and governments are legion, they appear inconscient in their purpose. Although we remain separated by credo and color, there is a growing global community that finds us deeply longing for a pacific world of social order. Through our collective force, which can be found in the wellspring of cultural exchange, there is the great potential to unite our energies and send a beacon of congruent truth, a ray of wisdom, from the inner sanctum of self-awareness to the external world of our everyday experiences.

Man indeed lives with a profound desire to understand himself and to evolve beyond the sentient creature that carries the punishing weight of fear. He navigates circuitously through frozen social patterns and carries the weighted atlas of emotional confusion. An ordering of histrionics identifies his demeanor, and his behavior expresses itself through a pattern of affairs which moves along precise channels joining individuals outwardly in a technically functioning community, but not inwardly from the historicity of their souls.

In an attempt to reduce the stigma of self-doubt modern man has developed a frail, but lasting bond with his fellow man, which is based considerably more on bartering and less so on a genuine and verdant handshake. Man imagines via his domination of so called "lower animals", and then again through his formidable manipulation of inert matter, that he has reached some conclusive level of superiority. He forgets the empathy clinging between man and beast, except when he looks up from reading his favorite book and watches as his dog sleeps, huddled by the fireplace, and then his creature-companion suddenly awakens to glance up and affectionately sigh, and then falls back to his peaceful and 'twitching' slumber.

He disregards the intimate connection between human and animal, except when he calls to his dog, not once but twice, and in the distance from the high grass, views his animal-friend leaping and straining to meet his own eyes. In these moments his humanness is discovered when he catches his reflection in the eye of one who is not human.

The same recognition seems to have vanished between human beings whose only hold on 'connectedness' lies in a hypothetical interdependence. The disparaging effects of modern preoccupations and cultural interventions have side-lined man's capacity to contemplate the wonder of existence; prevented from seeing that the spreading ripple from a raindrop has indeed fallen from the inexpressible world of the natural.

The reaching for a peaceable approach in human inter-relatedness has had to face a formidable opponent and the adversary is our own obsession with knowledge, whereupon we have come to believe that this great ship of information, that we are still building, will take us from the inlet of ignorance and carry us to some final shore of authority.

In point of fact we have reached a conflict where our thirst for knowledge interferes directly with our search for personal serenity, and for a peace that cannot be found anywhere on earth. Most certainly, our technological advances, discoveries, and our gatherings of facts, have not led to any real happiness.

The mighty coin of evolution was tossed before the dawn of thought and here we find ourselves treading the ancient currents that push against our ignorance. There exists a titanic dream to reach a higher plateau in human inter-relatedness and this vision has been charged, with great hope and emphasis, to the runnings of science.

We can see how technology has surged ahead of common reason, racing ever forward, flashing words at the speed of light. It peers with cycloptic precision beyond trillions of miles of space. Its formidable weapons stagger emotional comprehension and it proceeds with buoyant optimism into the twenty-first century planning air-routes for sky-cars that will make road-maps obsolete.

It has established unimaginable wealth and at the same time has widened the gap between classes of people, having created a distressing dichotomy with clear lines drawn between those who are jaded by comfort and those whose eyes are hollow with hunger.

However it may be, the knowledge that has evolved to become 'Science' was invented by Man and science is therefore human.

We appear to be living amidst a superfluous mosaic of formidable fragments belonging to what has been seen as the great scientific revolution. Certainly, a great light has been shed upon distressing and violent circumstances that have plagued man in our twentieth century and considerable good has turned the dark pages of our evolution.

Yet the way to serenity lies distant and strained and the way to peace lies inexpressibly desolate and costly for man to follow.

In the end, knowledge attains its full meaning only through the bond which unites mankind and not because man can master what is concretely knowable.

Trials, tribulations, and obstacles form the theater of events that in the end manage to shape the fabric of human experience. The ultimate objective is to enlarge our conceptual framework and embrace a methodology which springs forth from the ground of a universal 'consciousness-of-being.'

We can see that our outward actions, despite guile and genius, have not quelled our fears and uncertainties.

Our real aim need be in the development of a cognizance which will bear the fruit of a more total revelation of one's **real** purpose; an awareness which will fill the individual life with the strength of self-comprehension.

The journey of 'consciousness' is an ascent to a choate awareness that will cut through the inaccessible rigidity found in modern man's lopsided intellectual posture, and finally reach a closure in the awkwardness of his emotional temperament. Europe, America and other countries which compose the free world are living a hypocritical, graceless existence. We do not see a life that is free, unconventional, joyous, or unprejudiced. We do not feel the liberty of love, or the triumphant variety of passion. There exist only lies - lies to oneself and to others, lies about everything that we recognize in our hearts to be true.

We feel required to pretend affectation for people and respect for institutions we think ludicrous. We live fastened in a timidly fashion to moral and social conventions we spurn, denounce, and know lack all endowment.

The gross insufficiency of human inter-relatedness has propelled the encumbered individual to seek a more isolated position that will minimize his exposure to what has become "apprehension in the face of communication". This level of anxiety has caused a retreat into a private compartment that will safeguard the individual's *odyssey in fear*. Some small measure of success has been attained through the setting of a self-enclosed reality and creating a walled-in personal climate that will grant imagined self-protection. After all is said and done, this equivocal sojourn is an escape, and we can see how the individual has driven himself into a forest of corporeal comforts so as to mute the actuality of his self-isolation. His 'material' ingression is supported by the agency of technical devices belonging to the 'modern age' which drag him still further away from his capacity for human inter-relatedness, and he remains misled by a parade of endless inventions that fill the staleness of his solitude.

The attempt is to remain sequestered in a wealth of technical paraphernalia, that awaits his order, and to stay hidden away inside the reclusive borders of a prefabricated reality, which reveals his resignation. In the final analysis, the substance of existence is to be found along a circumventive trail that is considerably poor in emotional content. This is the individual refuge, which is after all, nothing more than a flight to a temporal asylum.

In his self-imposed emotional solitude, and in his undeclared loneliness, the individual loses himself to a delusional departure in mechanical reality which protects him only from an intimacy which can nurture his soul. He is left to his inbred devices and can only call upon utilitarian measures to shield what feels to be a vulnerable exposure to his emotional disconnection.

Tied together, the nameless and the faceless, gather in the manipulation of materials which only serve to further the interests of scientific avarice and the cold calculations of technological criteria.

The need for mastery, in the face of fear and inadequacy, is assuaged by man's glorious claims to victory over what was once a 'primitive' life. His insatiable need for power and control had long ago occasioned him to slave-holding other animals so as to undertake the duties and labors of his requirements through life. This ruthless level of domination, which in a truer sense is enslavement, remains unchanged, and in the end has decimated animal populations with the toll growing ever closer to the extinction of the precious diversity of living beings that collectively identify the planet Earth. This is not so much a defense for ignorant animals and insentient creatures but reveals an attitude of criminality and exposes his bloodthirsty under-takings.

Despite these atrocious defilements, he believes he has reached a formidable scientific advantage, and yet what is becoming more apparent is that his triumphs have frequently been at odds with his yearning for emotional peace.

All in all, history has shown man to be a self-serving creature capable of both great invention and great cruelty. Yes, Man has a reached a degree of 'superiority' in which he is at formidable odds with himself, his fellow man, and finally with nature.

Walking the technological line between marvel and horror, he has managed to separate himself even further from the universe which is his home.

"The human race is not truly great by the asset of its arms, it is great by its use of science, and above all by its arts."

He tosses the evolutionary coin into the air; the obverse and reverse of the same issue reveals grand achievement and also demonstrates his malevolence respectively.

The real direction for the human soul can be found in the development of 'mindfulness,' and the journey is to be ultimately free from the muted and dampened emotions which prohibit creative and spontaneous self-enterprise. This freedom will be found when there is an altogether cutting away of the oppressive uncertainty that clings to the guarded feelings that hinder real communication.

This emotional conundrum lies at the heart of our social problems and through the wisdom of the ages, as can be found in the Tai Chi philosophy, there is known to exist an "ascension of being" that will allow the individual to sail with greater fluency along the rising-and-falling sea of human inter-relatedness and plunge into the waters of self-comprehension.

From Man's meager beginnings, set against the red sky of the early dawn of time, where fur and bone protected him from an inhospitable environment, to the designed artifacts and devices of modern times, his race continues to exist because of his capacity to dream. And the visions that have risen from his 'dreaming' have led to significant discoveries. And with each breakthrough Man has grown ever more fervent in his desire to know himself.

We have sat at the great loom of life and weaved a tale of both mystery and mayhem, and the dye we have chosen reveals the inelegant color of reality that we have single-handedly fabricated.

Can we call upon the prodigious gift of awareness to change the trials of uncertainty? Can we spin the wondrous wheel of mind and shape yet another paradigm that will palliate our uneasiness? Or, shall will we sit under the great tree of knowledge, never having achieved a real understanding of the life we live, wading through the caliginous waters of self-doubt, while continuing in our mistrust of human intention which has accompanied our journey in human evolution for hundreds of thousands of years?

Then we turn our heads with the weight of lore and listen to the far-off thunder of self-reality announcing the heavenly 'storms of awareness', which could be released . . . but which are not yet.

"*The far-off thunder of self-reality announces the storms of awareness, which could be released, but which are not yet.*"

Beyond Survival

"My fearsome journey would never be ended.
Lost in a labyrinth, I should tread the valley
forever."

— Gertrude Bacon

To comprehend the meaning of life is to twist
and wind our way through the labyrinth of the mind.
Along the extensive and dusky corridors we view the
doors to Man's shadowy development. We stop at a
doorway that opens to the story of human evolution;
an evolvement which has been molded by
psychological dilemmas.

The signpost reads; "We are what our thoughts
have made us and as we think so we become!"

Indeed, man is defined by his ability to think.
Nevertheless, where there is thought there are
varying degrees of tension.

In point of fact, tensity is the mainspring of our
awareness and governs our intellective watchfulness.
The tension associated with mental calculation is
necessary if we are to arrive at solutions to the vast

array of problems which confront us daily. Nevertheless, as questions and issues mount, more often our ability to keep pace diminishes.

The pendulum swings in harmony only as long as we are mindful of the appropriate degree of tension needed to maintain the biophysical clock's internal balance. Too much or too little and we are out of 'synch' with our ability to judge what is right and what is wrong.

If the mind is engaged in a perpetual output of energy and fails to respect and honor a time for stillness and self-composure, this distorted expenditure of personal energy can only lead to a state of exhaustion that will ultimately interfere with perception and precision.

The key to fine-tuning the mainspring of tension can be found in the criterion related to the 'conservation of energy', i.e. "to protect energy leads to the building and availing of energy". In addition, the right interaction of tension and relaxation leads to a condition which augments physical stamina, and enhances mental energy.

Many people are caught on the 'wheel-of-anxiety,' wherein the desire to be released from aberrated tensions is attended by inexact and erroneous methods of relaxation. The vast majority of so-called "health-building" approaches have surfaced prematurely, in that they are oftentimes anchored to miscalculated findings and commercial self-interest.

This points to the domain of quick-fix-parlor-tricks claiming youthful rejuvenation, miracle fat-burning and weight-reduction, all of which are 'snake-oiled' to a naive and gullible public.

Genetic predisposition, eating habits, and the general condition of the consumer are rarely taken into consideration; and these 'slippery methods'

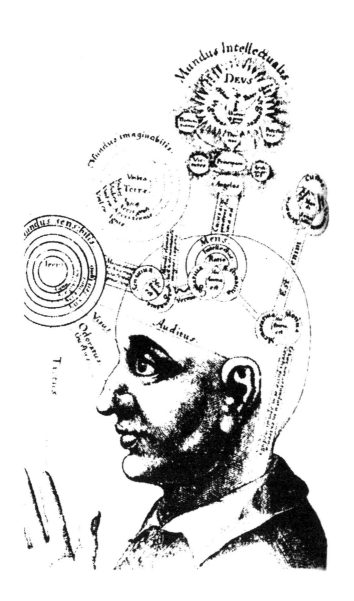

succeed in driving us away from taking responsibility for our own well-being by supplying us with miracle cures and 'instantaneous results,' as though 'any' exercise system or pill could possibly stand up to bad eating habits that are married to tiresome and spiritless exercising, to say nothing of the side-effects of tampering with enzymatic, metabolic, and hormonal factors.

The vast majority of these furtive approaches remove a person's ability to innovatively choose, for example, a healthful diet, or the appropriate exercise that conforms to the skills or demands that fall in line with an individual's personal and creative needs.

Ironically, many of these novel 'methods' close-off the restorative powers of our 'natural' healing capabilities, and we are left to the designs of unproved remedies and suspect equipment. In the end we are exposed to deciduous systems that close the door to the benefits of authentic approaches.

The dilemma that confronts the student is how to separate the cream from the curd, which happens to be lumped in the same misleading 'health-care' category.

Further still, there is the troublesome reality of a self-denigrating affair in which many spend precious energy on developing an 'image' at the expense of their health.

In the final analysis it appears that it is our *image of expectation* that seems to count. That is to say - self-validation is dependent upon other people's approval. Our sense of worth is tied up and reflected in the 'eyes of others.'

Beneath our *portrayal* remains the same chronic physical and psychic armoring which has paralyzed our dynamic potential; a state that grew out of our belief that personal actions are based on other people's endorsement of our conduct.

In order to return to a sense of wholeness, our attitude needs to begin with increasing our ability to manage personal energy more efficiently and in creating a dynamic ambiance for self-direction. What principally needs to be avoided is segregating physical and mental components.

Indeed, it is quintessential to recognize that 'wholeness' is determined by engaging the mind **and** body to work in concert. The energies of body and mind require integration and need to work in confluence, otherwise the availing of personal energy and its great benefits will fall by the wayside.

The danger in underestimating the synchronous relationship between body and mind, or underrating the solidarity of mental and physical acts, or the lack of it, is that we will be left with what amounts to a stifled influx of healing and creative energy that is so vital to our capacity for experiencing life in full measure.

Paying attention to physical strength alone is a lopsided approach to complete health and equally so when applied to the development of purely mental power. Physical and mental energy remain co-dependent, otherwise we may expect that the collective tensions which are cumulative in nature, will further impose their negative power on the emotional and psychological elements related to human health and development.

What is most encouraging is that there is available a system of learning that teaches us how to conserve and appropriate those energies that come from the 'inner-well' of human strength and instructs us in how to draw from the storehouse of creative energy that underlies the **mechanical** order of events that compose our thoughts and activities.

Can we break free of our relentless mind-wanderings that are made up of turbulent thoughts, criticisms and accusations? Can we transcend our justifications and recriminations? What is the effect on the health of mind and body when we perpetuate a host of frenzied impulses without respite or self-understanding?

It is our own self-undoing when we gather negative impulses, and it is the pouring out of negativistic emotions that ultimately eternalizes our inveterate and mechanistic behavior. We move through life having gotten accustomed to specious conduct and insincere behavior which in turn has become the modus vivendi of social intercourse.

This is the domain of ineluctable habits that act as detrimental propellants, driving surreptitiously through the actions of our lives.

We are left to the workings of our intractable responses that move through the familiar circle of everyday existence, as if life were nothing more than a stuttering ambulation, like a musical phrase being repeated by a phonograph with its needle caught in the groove! We need ask ourselves, in all sincerity, if the order of long standing tensions can be truly transcended without the wise counsel of joining the energies of body and mind.

Yes, modern man lives with deep-seated tensions and these collective encumbrances are demonstrated in a misaligned and faulty body-carriage, exhibited in a shallow breathing rhythm, and further evidenced in an urgent and strained mind-set.

These enervations and impairments literally suffocate his psychological and metabolic capacities and the whole of who he is comes to be expressed in a clamorous mentality, as well as in a forced, self-conscious demeanor.

How difficult it is to imagine that an individual so disposed can be set free from such disturbing debilitations once they have become so deeply implanted!

These 'mind-knots' evoke a loss in adaptability of functional performance and chain the individual to the fixed sequence of events as dictated by the handicapped ego.

As we peer into the historical past, the **ego** in ancient Greece was known as the 'persona' which was in fact a material **mask** that the actor wore in conformity to the elements of comedy or tragedy. The visage they created covered the entire head and although lacking distinct features was painted on linen cloth. The face came across as an eerie and faint signal that was however powerfully amplified from within the depths of mood, or madness, expertly dramatized by the actor.

We can plainly see the semantical evolution of persona to the word 'personal,' which in the scheme of events is in effect a betrayal of what the self is in fact.

Take for example the following statement; "I'd like to share something **personal** with you!"

This is something we have all said at one time or another and has a double-edge to its meaning when seen in the ancient light of Greek drama, and which curiously lies at the heart of the word 'personality.'

By sheer definition personality is registered as "something not one's own." However it may be, in the course of life the individual develops, if not one, then several personas, and the kind of masks that come to be developed are gradually formed by the kinds of relationships that we have with the people we are closest to; from our parents and siblings, to our teachers in school, our relatives and friends, including athletic groups and social clubs, and all are grist for the persona's mill.

Our free powers are checked by a weighty predicament in the passage of emotional time in that we cannot decide what *role* we care, or need to play, given the events in the theatre of modern life!

When we turn our heads on a certain angle we may have cause to see that society is composed of a strange medley of human beings who customarily participate in a social masquerade. No one is actually deceived by the games that are played in the pseudo-atmosphere of unemployed literary pretensions, political ambitiousness, theatrical snobbery, journalistic debauchery and high-heeled facetiousness.

But, each person finds it incumbent, in order to exalt himself, to glorify a notoriously platitudinous environment. Trite phrases and triviality attend the "tea-party" of social intercourse in which many find, not only a barely mentionable sustenance, but verily their only explanation for being.

The questions that grate against our sense of effectiveness, and often safety, may be posed in this manner; "What is the appropriate mask for the situation in hand that will help me succeed in my venturings?"

Success is the operative word, rather than 'intimacy,' and some have gone to great lengths to develop the marvelous faculty of being able to speak for hours on end, and on varied subjects, without expressing an idea.

There 'the actor' stands in the middle of some smoky hallway pouring forth a lexicon of contentious gibberish, as we brace ourselves for a quenchless rhetoric that sputters ceaselessly and untiringly in a languid, monotonous and decapitating torrent of philosophical, or if necessary, political vocabulary.

We swallow the frightful drama, our minds a whirling mass in dread-stricken disorder, but still we collaborate vigorously when the occasion finally presents itself and respond from our overused and stale word-stock in an awkwardly skeptical tone. We are ultimately exposed as an enthusiast empty of inspiration; a devotee devoid of spontaneity.

Later, we wash off the smoke and cologne, remove our make-up and lipstick, hang away our jackets and dresses, and crawl into bed, our heads bulging with noise, our brains swollen with invisible voices and alcohol. Prostrate, the continual oscillation of personal impotency and frenzy pervades our need for sleep.

The oppressive odor of the evening still clings to us, turning our stomachs with vagrant images pressing against our debilitated senses. Finally comes the twitch of sleep, and a pitiful defeat covers our growing slumber; a falling trance which reminds us of our extraordinary endurance to carry on without nourishment.

Cerebral congestion is attended by a fountain void of intuition that pours into yet another question; "Which persona shall I display so as to feel less uncomfortable?" The energy that is placed on the crafting of a mask remains hidden in the muffled texture of conformity whereupon we learn to play some roles fairly well, some which do not suit us, and others we cannot manage to play.

The particular role we have devised, or taken on, for better or worse, becomes the medium for our bodily demonstrations, facial expressions, vocal quality, turns of speech and opinions.

These collective elements maintain themselves through patterns of habit acquired through the many years of imitation, as well as through the commonplace occurrences and otherwise imposed circumstances taken in the mechanical stride of social life.

Like a weed growing steadily, while strangling the larger tree, the misrepresented individual, or false ego, if you will, progressively takes over the entire structure of the self. The essence of the individual is lost to the devices of egotistical delusions, negative emotions, self-pity, lies and posturings.

Here we wait hoping to be stripped of the artifices and hypocrisies with which the civilized world veils the real person.

The formidable ego stalks with liquid devices and slips beneath the waters of conscious reality, moving to rob the soul of whole experiences. And yet ironically, the ego stands as our delegate in the dimensional framework of experiential phenomena.

Like the snail without a home, requiring an outer shell so as to continue its journey in the unpredictable world of temporal events, so does the individual ego take on the 'sine qua non' masks of manipulation and play at the games necessary for survival in the mercurial realm of everyday urban encounters.

Evidence the magnificent poetic lecture belonging to the mind of English novelist D. H. Lawrence when he wrote these thoughts at the turn of the century;

"When we get out of the glass bottles of
*   our ego,*

and when we escape like squirrels
*   turning in the cages of*
*   our personality*

and get into the forests again,

we shall shiver with cold and fright

but things will happen to us

so that we don't know ourselves.

Cool, unlying life will rush in,

and passion will make our bodies taught
*   with power,*

we shall stamp our feet with new power

and old things will fall down,

we shall laugh, and institutions will curl up
*   like burnt paper. "*

Below the surface of the ego's varied performances, the **real** self is immobilized in a palisade of detached emotions and resigned to an infinity of excuses for the failures and weaknesses of the hour at hand.

In order to withstand the abuse, inadequacies and defeats of daily experiences, the central project confronting the individual is in the creation of a personality, or personas as it were, that will come to the rescue.

Sadly, who one truly is, remains securely fastened to the devices of the fabricated self, and gone is the **being** behind the project. The 'characters' so developed, in what amounts to a kind of self-deception, mobilize through a strategy of conduct that **acts** utterly for acquisition, esteem, admiration and absurdly drives towards **intimacy**.

But **who** is it that receives these rewards?

The awareness of 'being-what-one-is,' is repressed, but not without being somewhat conscious of its activity. Tragically one mendacious hand washes another and the automated-self is prepared and ready for confirming yet another person's lies.

In the end, it is a hiding from oneself so as not to face the troubled and unstable circumstances that make up the moments of reality.

The ego is well-schooled in facade and is engaged in an exercise of observing the truth in order to better conceal its stratagems more carefully. It reaches a proportion where it becomes a stable, albeit artificial platform for further adventures in the historicity of individual existence. Self-deception is a making of behavior to make up reality!

The 'reality' in question is formed by one's word, which often enough will not be kept; attitudes, that will appear in contradiction, and even promises that will frequently be broken. But nevertheless, this dire comportment constitutes a reality, if not a 'kind of truth.'

Somewhere between the thin line that separates falsehood from self-deception there exists a plethora of excuses and rationalizations that will serve the ego's mendacity, and these collective justifications will act to soften the uncomfortable reality that betrays the liar; the prevaricator who is, in actuality, in complete possession of the truth.

The veiled activities are summed up in the projects of the ego which has twisted reality and is bent on perpetuating its thin disguises. This theater of events has been established in defense of seeing what deceptions, or lies, the ego cares to hold on to, and so to make its way through the parade of confusion that marks the boundaries of emotional content.

As Jean Paul Sartre questioned; "What is the nature of man if he is *capable* of self-deception?"

Paradoxically, the ego appears to be a necessary evil in the hustle and bustle of society's 'survival strategy' as related to the trials of the modern city, or dare I say, the tragedy of modernity. The assemblage of the ego is an adaptation that helps the individual fit into his environment, just as a tiger's stripes render the animal invisible in the tall jungle grass.

Analogously, to accomplish our ends we have also 'disappeared' and that is to say, the inner-self has made a rather difficult adjustment; we have become actors, impersonators, performers, and role-players. Without pretending melodrama we have often felt and responded in a fashion so described; "I live and breathe, but in an entirely different fashion that has come to be disquietingly familiar, yet horribly necessary." And again; "I exist through a cadged history supported by a wardrobe of masks that of necessity I will choose from daily in order to adapt and accommodate, if not to conform, to the rigors of social, business and private intercourse."

For many, we have become cynical enough to adopt a chimerical character and play out a hypocritical charade so as to endure the vicissitudes of the world today and its social pecking order. Indeed, we scrupulously *mutate* as we move about

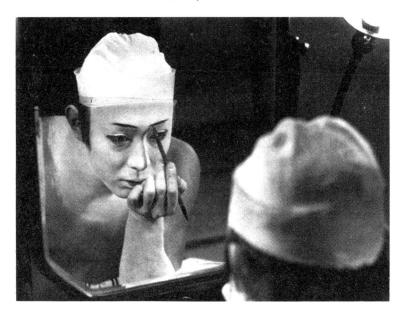

"We want to remove the mask of falsity, but a part of our disguise still clings to us."

from one world to another in the daily round of living. We modify our behavior as we dart from the office or studio to the gym or club. We take on the role of the boss, or being bossed, and remodel ourselves as we transform our image to one of an athlete or artist.

We alter our feelings as we enter our homes and the mask is transfigured when we act as the parent and approach our children, and then guilefully recast ourselves when we confront our own parents.

By the end of the day the masks are set aside, but the fictive weight is not so easily dropped, even when we join with a trusted partner!

Life is reduced to a shifting series of pretended roles and relationships in what amounts to aching, emotional bankruptcy.

Our framework for living is wrapped up in our middle-class anxiety, immediate material concerns, fearful desires, anxious dreams and disappointments. We are living in a reduced cosmos where we are actually making contact with only 'parts' of ourselves and with mere parts of other people. In the end who and what we are is represented by our relations to others and life is sadly given over to dispirited intentions that radiate through pretentious acts and mundane behavior.

This is the nature of the ego and demonstrates the quality and condition of human existence that has been pushed into the temporal flux of half-truths. It is an escape from *oneself* expressed as; "I leave the garment of my disguise on the playing field of evasion." Or; "I am driven by my need to be that which-is-for-others and yet I am possessed by the need to be that which-is-myself!"

After all, can impersonation be seen as a way of expanding our identities and enriching our lives?

Indeed, we dare not let those feelings that come from the depths of the *inner-self* disturb our precarious balance. There are some memories of who we are and of which we are dimly aware, but we never allow ourselves to become entirely conscious of the whole of the circumstances which bind us to the charade. In the end our lives become the product of our own distorted awareness.

The elusive self is indeed divided! We feel fractured and separated into disjointed entities and dissimilar parts, with disparate voices and fragmented identities; all seeking attention and at the same time, respite.

Regrettably, each of these voices command the moment and remain in distant and strained relation to each other. This mix of characters expresses marked differences in organization, offering different explanations and solutions, and often enough in argumentative opposition to one another.

Put into motion is a calamity within the framework of the individual's emotional content. Here within the fiasco of obtuse reality, consciousness appears like the surface of the ocean in a great storm, while the mind can no more hold on to simple awareness than the captain of a ship who is being battered by a hurricane can engage in the writing of his sea-log.

We find the mind strewn about in a sea of deep perplexion and we remain ignorant as to who we are and blind to where we are heading. Sadly we discover that we do not know the acts or operations expected of us, and we may grandly exclaim; "I submerge my personality in the mechanical compulsions of my job, or in an equally mechanistic association to a society of concussive reductionists."

We stare dumbfounded into the dark pool of self-reflection!

We want to remove the mask of falsity and unveil what is real, but through some misdeed, perhaps through some miscalculation, a part of our disguise still clings to us; a hint of self-importance endures in our raised eyebrow; a curl of self-flattery remains in our hair. We must not see the lines of exaggeration in the corners of our mouth, as we spew forth the contents of a conversation that is only a shallow word-game belonging to an intellectual puzzle that aborts sincerity.

And so we amble circuitously, an imitation of something we imagine worthwhile and we succumb to the farce, neither having achieved being a half of who we are, nor as it is said, even being good actors.

When seen through the many eyes of our varied personalities, life takes on a defenseless and confusing quality, a roughened texture which negates our sense of truth and obstructs our capacity, even our desire, to let life fall into a more gentle and irenic place.

This is the theater of affairs, the arena of conflict, where the real enemy is the rehearsed, negative, and impatient self within.

Will the individual come to see the flaw in the logic of what amounts to a schizoid's dream-world? Can the individual move beyond the nervous and sycophantic smile that has come to replace sincerity?

Can we drop our irrational mechanisms and measure our lives by the validity of the feelings which belong to our inner-self? Will we reach beyond a "personality" that has been manufactured by a tissue of fabrication which temporally suits the 'social situation'? Can we ever return to a state of 'being-what-one-is'?

The web of cultural intervention must be judiciously negotiated if we want to elude its hold on our behavioral responses.

Using a Taoist strategy, we exert a Tai Chi move on our acquired, handed-down experience by means of which its force will be turned upon itself so that it can fall flat on its own impersonal face.

If we are to transcend then we must learn to *dance*! To understand the method we must begin by seeing that there are two worlds to dance in. There is the 'dance of life' in which our actions are spontaneous and open, and penetrate to genuine feelings. It is a dance that we all cherish and romanticize about, and it is an idealized state which would allow us to step more lightly and sincerely through the world.

Then again there is the 'dance of the dead'! The difference between the two can be seen in the example of the 'dance of the waiter' in an outdoor café. His actions are nimble and fastidious, perhaps a little too exacting, and his steps a little too quick. He stands there, with his hands behind his back, with his head lowered to the height of the table top. He carries on, overly eager to please, making furtive glances as one ready to submit to torture. His voice is quietly raised in a kind of modest apology and there is an eagerness in his bend that outweighs the circumstances of an event, which after all, demands only the ordering of a meal. He bounces away with mechanical preciseness and eventually returns with the controlled rapidity of some kind of automaton. The tray is handled with a juggler's sense of perpetual instability and his movements drive between the tables with the controlled recklessness of one navigating a canoe through rapids.

All his maneuvers appear to us like some 'put-on,' and he dances around as he plays the game of a 'waiter.' He must limit his function to being subservient, only daring to be a servant and surely not a human being like those who study his antics out of the corner of their critical eye.

Certainly, we are not permitted to know that the waiter is tired, or upset, or concerned about his sick child.

But wait a moment, there is someone else in the café, sitting in a far corner - someone you almost missed, sitting slumped in the chair with a dull and far-away look in her eyes — the shoulders quietly fallen, hands clasped together in her lap, her head lowered, staring down at them; those trembling hands that seem almost as though they are praying, hoping that no one will see the sadness, the deep sorrow that is welling up from inside her hurt.

It looks a lot like you, once upon a time, and you know that you will not be able to hold on to this dysphoria, because the waiter will be sauntering by to refill your cup, or ask if he can get you "Anything else?," and you don't know if the river of tears that you are holding back will unexpectedly rush forth like a torrent and expose you in front of him or the others who may be close enough.

You will have to postpone your sadness!

How absurd that you must delay your right to be yourself because "the waiter is here!" And you will save your tears for later, when the waiter is gone, and for now you lift your head and quickly paint a smile on your face, while your heart is wrenching. And again in the silence of your own dilemma it comes to you, as you force your lips to move politely in the direction of the waiter, and as though nothing in the world could be wrong.

You think to yourself; "To be what I really am in this terrible and precious moment is impossible . . . because . . . ?"

And so the account proceeds as the 'dance of the dead' continues, and the events of life make themselves felt on all of us.

In this frivolous and often desperate game, the public will make their demands, acting as they are in their necessary roles, which certainly must **never** be confused with insincerity. There they struggle unknowingly, with the invisible twitch of self-mockery, trapped in the mode of being what **they** are not!

So it is, as well, for the grocer who paces his narrow lair behind the counter and must withstand the prison of his own servile attitude, reinforced as it were, by the oppressive requirements of his clientele.

Then again there is the bus driver who sits out his time offering a ticket in place of a simple handshake. What of the soldier who must remain assured within the confines of his rock-bound rigidity and guise and who dares not dream of the kind of clothes that will make him seem like any other man.

There they are, all of them, no longer meant to see beyond their part, and to be none other than the role they play in the drama of affairs.

This calculated game, requires that we all play at being what-we-are-not, and finally to settle for acting out the rights and duties of our "position" in society's sketchy game of propriety.

With all the emphasis placed on outward platitudes and material concerns, we have forgotten that there is an inward journey; we might say, an intrepid journey that carries to a more gentle space, a safer place, where worlds no longer collide. We face the future, waiting for a glimpse, a sign, that will paint a picture of self-harmony. We anticipate halcyon days that breathe with a bouquet of natural synchrony.

But for now, we uncover a grating reality and find ourselves painting with halting strokes on nature's antique canvas which exposes the many faces of man; overlapping portraits that beautify and likenesses that horrify.

We are in the gallery of human evolution and our knowledge has grown to a point where we have a real chance to view a more complete picture of man and one that reveals, perhaps painfully, the disparate masks and inconscient personalities we all have come to wear.

"Man reveals himself through actions that beautify and deeds that horrify."

Tai Chi points with elevated reason to a higher platform of awareness that speaks of evolving beyond the boundaries imposed by the 'personality' which has been shaped by the pretexts and predilections of our immediate culture. Its teachings reach further than the present range of events as undergone in the arena of 'society'; a society that has placed material concerns far too forward of the rest of life's experiences.

The uncomfortable picture is one of myopic striving. In our efforts and vision to reach higher standards of social and cultural excellence, we have become obsessed with winning and competition. We have been seduced by the outer appearance of goals and attainment. Our deliberations have grossly interfered with our natural rhythm, our natural self-hood, and we have brought upon ourselves the various stresses and pathologies which threaten individual health and well-being.

The ramifications point clearly to the blight of damaging effects that are being imposed on the progeny of future generations.

The heirs of the modern world are being denied access to a more complete understanding of man's capacity to find self-harmony without the disproportionate reliance on material affluence.

In our attempt to keep pace with the velocities of the modern city, we have taken on a psychological posture, a precarious emotional stance, if you will, which finds expression in aberrant displays of specious actions and false expressions.

Here is the modus operandi of our own **self-undoing**. It is testament to an anomalous development which stands in contrariety to our inherent naturalness.

The nature of man's disjointedness can be traced to the misappropriation of personal energy, on both physical and mental levels, which has lead to profoundly rooted tensions that have become displaced in a myriad of physiological and psychological ailments.

Many solutions to vibrant health have come and gone, while some are being invented, and still others are being reinvented. That we have so far not succeeded only points to the truth of our continuing in an attitude of placing the body before mind, or the mind before body. Whether any one of these methods will begin to approach the problems that we face in our Information Age will be determined by their capacity to recognize the confluence of the mind/body relationship.

The connection between mind and body has intrigued the Chinese for millennia and traditional Chinese medicine has recognized the relationship between mental and physical aspects of disease for nearly five thousand years. Through the effective modalities found in the Tai Chi methodology, physiological and psychological integration is highlighted. This celebrated method of approach enlists the mind to direct the energies of the body and allows the diverse organic functions to operate in harmony. Special detail is paid to the unification of upper and lower body dynamics as it relates to movement and in its positive effects on overall health.

What is artfully underscored is the synchronous communication between mental and physical operations. This is certainly a more balanced approach which stands in contradistinction to our engrossment with the upper dimensions of the body, particularly the head, which has come about through intellectual pursuits that are tied to skills related to hand and speech.

Indeed, because of the preoccupation with intellectual dynamics, modern man has transferred his sense of power from the true physical center of the body, to the top of the body. We have moved away from seeing the whole of who we are and are literally rushing 'a-head' of who we are!

"Chinese medicine recognized the mind/body connection nearly 5000 years ago."

This 'rush to control' is exhibited in the contemporary attitude of struggling to shrink time and modify space. This incentive pursues a course in reason that hopes to somehow make room for life. It is a colossal effort which is consistently side-lined through an ever salacious desire for power and material comfort.

Generalship is required in the war waged on human intelligence and well-being, and we must become aware of the double-agent within the ranks who commands from the glossy towers of our industrial and commercial edifices.

Below the looming spires we scurry about, "keeping busy," as they say, so as to avoid the glare of self-destruction. This slapdash attitude is better seen as an anxious effort to 'get ahead' and nevertheless interferes and defeats its own object.

After all, what is the value of acquisition without the possession of a healthy mind? What is power without a well-tuned body to appreciate delights of the sensorium?

Anxiety, or stress, produces psychological and physiological strains, and strain is incompatible with the proper means for achieving our goals!

The prominent Chinese philosopher and statesman, known as Kung-Fu-Tse, popularly referred to as Confucius, coined the phrase, "A thousand mile journey begins with a single step!" It is not how many steps you can take that counts, it is the quality of the steps you take which insures the character of your well-being and underscores the essence of who you are in the patterns of your life.

As a nation of people we have become a crowded network of near automatons and our movements are made of ceaseless wanderings that dream outside of nature's laws. We are directed by the abnormal appetites of endless consumption and proceed with cravings for spurious adventure which, in and of itself, reveals an emptiness in the quality of our experiences. We have buried ourselves in ambitious enterprise and have created an unbalanced approach in living, having placed our emotional development second to the victory over material concerns. By some bizarre emotional calculation we have grown accustomed to the mechanical operations of the social 'work-zone' and have become addicted to ephemeral pleasures, and finally to the acquirement of power.

"We have become a crowded network of near-automatons that dream outside of nature's laws."

However it may be, the 'payoff' is felt in the halting and sometimes crippling effects imposed on our nervous system.

How difficult it is to imagine that we can be extricated from these debilitating neurological and physiological entanglements which are so powerfully reinforced by the contumacious demands of commercial enterprise and marketing approaches.

The envelope of existence is being pushed to its limit by the social pressures for material success!

The various stresses of life, whether they be physical strain or psychological frustration, and then again emotional distress, can all be gathered under the heading of 'tension.'

It is here, in the realm of tensity, that we find the bog of human 'dis-ease.' This is where the die is cast! This is the fettered frontier that forges the mettle of man, and society is the theater of conflict where man is cast and re-cast.

We have all entered this **battle**, so to speak, related to our own perception and often distorted view of reality, and have developed various strategies and approaches in an attempt to buffer the stresses that accompany the encounters which make up the weighted events of life.

One such method, unacquainted with it as we may be here in the West, concerns the articulations of 'Tai Chi'; a system of learning which develops and engages a full range of psychological and physical responses belonging to our 'whole sense of being.' Through its plan of action we become involved in creating a miniature cosmos with an emphasis on mental focus and self-composure. The power of this system is built on a platform of artful demands made on body **and** mind.

As we progress we acquire renewed vitality and heightened awareness, whereupon we can then take our earned strength and clarity and deal more effectively and intelligibly with the outer activities, as well as the inner events, belonging to our daily round of affairs. Certainly, we need to honor the nature of our involvements in the affairs of social and personal intercourse, and to carry forward in this respect we need to recognize the importance of the quality of 'being' we possess, which in turn enlivens or deadens our capacity for genuine communication and human intimacy. Tai Chi points to the meritorious quality of being 'real;' a realness that would flow into the movements of all our encounters, today and tomorrow.

In Tai Chi we are creating a novel set of parameters in a new world of personal order, not only for the body, but for the mind as well. The real effort is to begin to work on the control of attentive awareness, for there is little else that is more valuable to our movement through life than clarity of mind.

In the words of C.W. Wendte; "Success in life is a matter not so much of talent and opportunity, as of concentration and perseverance!"

Although taken for granted, mental energy is not only limited, but is in perpetual adjustment, and is no different than the energy which supports our muscular functions, with the accompanying highs and lows expressed in cycles that have stronger and weaker periods.

Furthermore, it is within our command to squander this vital resource, or to wisely conserve it. Whether it happens to be a floating thought, like a mind-tune in repetitive cadence; a passing impression received from a bill-board caught from inside our moving vehicle; perhaps a sudden noise in a restaurant, or a piece of commercialized information that shouts at us as we stare into the bold face of our television sets; and then again rumored conversations that pervade the atmosphere in the vicinity of our office, we must begin to see that each of these runnings involves a reaction. And where there is stimulation, be it physical or mental, there is energy required to support it.

"Outward platitudes and material preoccupation have deadened our capacity for genuine human intimacy."

We can say that in fact there is a loss of energy, to one degree or another, and the energy that supports our awareness, once lost cannot be so easily reclaimed, since the human organism has only so much in reserve!

There are innumerable perceptions and stimuli that plunge into our awareness that merely serve as distractions and are too often accompanied by a legitimate draining of vital energy. If energy cannot be created, as science informs us, then perhaps it can be better preserved!

It is here upon the creative platform of Tai Chi that we learn to transfer the energy from the catabolic, or destructive phase, into the anabolic or creative state, in much the same way that the body manufactures energy-substances during the sleep phase that is to be used for vital functions during the waking phase. If we are to succeed in understanding "wholeness" and if we wish to make the best use of personal energy, we need to look upon the relationship of mind and body. And to do that, let us consider the 'moving-brain' which is in control of all our voluntary muscular exertions and an area which plays a significant role in the mental, or psychic realm as well.

As William James concluded in his impressive study of the mind-body connection; "The sensation of self is largely made up of muscular sensations concentrated in the facial region and especially the area of the lips." This evidence has been corroborated in neurological research on the brain.

To continue; there is an area of the brain called the **homunculus** which when prodded with electrical-field-stimulation, there comes about a concomitant muscular response. This excitation also reveals that the head and lips, (thinking/speaking), make up a considerably large area of representation along this centrally located topographical region.

Returning to Dr. James' related research, the symptoms of neurosis were seen to be dependent upon, or reinforced by muscular tension and could be relieved by the induction of relaxation.

The medical effectiveness of the Tai Chi method is constructed on a foundation of relaxation techniques which both stimulate and conserve the body's energy, keeping precious reserves for sundry uses and dramatically stabilizing nervous energy as well.

The high degree of coordination developed through Tai Chi practice points clearly to those faculties associated with the brain's moving-center.

As the student practices on the exercise platform, we can see the growth of complex and skillful articulations which become increasingly more substantial as the student evolves in his mind-body education. The maneuvers found in the Tai Chi choreography evolve from the simple to the complex and the finely crafted movements call upon the primordial center of the moving-brain to release its wisdom; sapience which was acquired through an evolutionary process spanning countless ages.

This is the same instinctive skill that flows from the moving center that animals have managed to hold on to despite our violations on their habitats. This is evidenced in the agility of the spider monkey darting through the tree-tops. Take the graceful running and turning-on-a-dime maneuvers of the cheetah as another prime example; as well as the counterbalanced soaring of the frigate bird on the updrafts of warm air.

The moving-brain extends its expressions in the rhythmic thunder of a galloping horse's hoof-beats, and the examples so far given here point to the modus operandi that reflects the quality of motion which identifies 'instinctive-intelligence,' and is the synchronous notation which rises from the primeval well of the moving-brain.

This is the same instinctive intelligence that the spider uses to build its intricate web, time after time, and in the same manner, the eagle goes about constructing its great wooden-nest. This study is equally applied to the tireless architecturalizing of the bee-hive and to the building of the distinct individual honey-combs. Then again there is the construction of the immovable dam of the beaver, as well as the silk-spinning magic of cocoons loomed by caterpillars.

All these foregoing examples are unique, varying in complexity and structural composition, yet all are extensions of the moving-brain's remarkable provision.

Tai Chi is a reeducation of the lost skills found in the moving-center and carries our awareness back to our bodies; to the muscles and tendons, to the ligaments, and even to the organs themselves. The craftwork found in the ingenious designs of the Tai Chi form-play offer the careful observer a wealth of material that will help the student rediscover the eloquence of the moving-brain.

This retraining will counterbalance the lopsided articulations of the thinking-brain which has been reinforced by our technical predilections and the modern gadgetry that in turn acts to bind the mind to purely intellectual criteria.

It is the preoccupation with technological tools and less so with physical skills and creative motion that has caused the moving-brain to atrophy.

With the demise of the moving-center we have lost the simple pleasure of graceful movement and the fine sense of coordination that speaks to us of simpler moments and natural gifts. For it was not long ago that man's entire social development was dependent on the 'handling' of materials and his livelihood was bound to manipulative skills. The strength, or lack of such dexterities, categorically shaped his living environment.

Social evolution was caught up in various crafting abilities, whether it was the construction of a schoolhouse, or the building of a bridge; muscles were the sole means for its completion. In fact, it was the way man made his living, as men, even today, carry on in traditions like fishing, carpentry, hunting and crop gathering; all of which are receding into the archaic.

Tai Chi is a return to those skills which keep us connected to the entirety of the human organism and especially to the motor functions.

What are we and how do we identify ourselves as unique individuals? What is it that makes us who we are?

To ascertain the identity of man is to take hold of his brain, which begins as a mass of flesh and blood and ends as a tangle of incomprehensible fears, dreams, visions and nightmares. What identifies man is consciousness, awareness if you will, which includes our ability to conjure and create realities that are initially based on an intellective plan, a mental scheme.

Maintaining a keenness of mind is another matter altogether!

For instance, there are times when we struggle to awaken in the morning, emerging from the dark passage of the unconscious, as it were, with a transient, but sometimes disturbing parade of conflicting images that returns us from our nightly 'disappearance.'

Somewhat dazed we lie in bed having risen from the dusky mist of encumbered sleep. We lie there, in that foggy instant, somewhere between full consciousness and utter unconsciousness, not knowing where or even who we are. The perplexity is ephemeral, but nevertheless carries the weight of the unknown; that tentative moment of uncertainty, if not alarm, when we awaken, in which we can't begin to imagine what became of us, and that we may have just as well been dead.

When rejoining full consciousness, there is a sigh of assurance in feeling the 'weight of our bodies.'

It is in this relatively disturbing moment, and then again, in the wonderful relief of finally and completely awakening, that we clearly see that the sensation of self is built into our muscular and skeletal structure.

The drama of sleep does not simply lie down and rest. Its web clings to our consciousness as perception becomes transposed to the waking movements of the day and we find ourselves pushed into the 'composed' framework of conscious awareness.

As it is, for most of us, these days, the actions which predominantly belonged to the physical realm are left to the devices of mental assignments and to the nervous motions which embody a typical work-day.

Today's drudgery is profoundly different from the antiquated days of simple, albeit difficult labor.

Men's course of action had been regulated fundamentally by the rhythms of nature and quite so his economic behavior. It was Nature that dictated, year to year, the kind of work which had to be pursued. The thrust of activities operated within the framework set by the seasons which offered fair and foul weather, and physical and mental energy alike was ordered by the subordinate divisions of light and darkness.

"Today's drudgery is profoundly different from the antiquated days of difficult labor."

Men were bonded to their animals and lived in great intimacy with their tools. They were united to their fields where they toiled with the kind of care a mother would spend on her growing child.

One bad harvest and the entire economy of a nation could be ruined!

Now we are surrounded with exotic machines and curious devices doing the work of a hundred laborers and in less time than the bygone worker would have spent in wiping his brow from sweat. The punishing weight of physical tasks that once occupied man's movement through life has been replaced by the digital calculations of gleaming circuits and switches no bigger than the period at the end of this sentence.

But the habits of centuries are not so easily lost, and in the 'civilized' world, the hotel house-keeper in her 'endless-bendings' knows herself to be little else than her muscles, as does, so painfully, the convalescing patient, as he pulls himself from his wheel-chair and locates the *self* through his musculature, or rather lack of it.

Now man uses his muscles in order to "stay fit" and for keeping the cardiovascular system strong, or building the legs and shaping the buttocks. The *merciful* hands of technology have relegated the activities of man's muscles to vainglorious preoccupations.

Even natural forms of exercise have been replaced by machines that almost walk for you, with sweating bicyclists and perspiring skiers "going" nowhere.

Witness the peculiar 'fitness-center' event of men with imaginary oars rowing about without water. Here is the realm of dramatic 'inertia' which blows upon the flame of self-expression.

With every new invention comes a gust of technological wind that will finally extinguish what is left of our creative and passionate involvement in knowing ourselves through body and mind.

We are left behind a cultural cordon where the application of 'tech-knowledge-y' already contains that kernel of dishonesty; for *it* dares to proceed to conquer our awareness of our entirety. It is as though we are being forced out of our own ability to reason, and technology, however grand it appears, is culpable of a philosophical violation that robs us of thoughtful reflection.

We can no longer quietly push-on in the continuity of an asymmetrical intellective vehicle for self-expression. It appears that we are left, as it were, to swim in an endless sea of quantifiable facts, nuanced by our struggle to keep up with the sordid climb for more information, more equipment, and more of what turns out to be theatrical boredom.

The entire miscellany is punctuated with the irritation of our hunting and pecking amongst the cold calculations of statistical rubble. We are banished to the maddening inventory of geometric and intellectual adventures of hypnotic perspectives that merely allow us to dream life without living it. We are left to the *abstract* which never interprets emotion and rather disintegrates into a realm of existence inhabited by shapes that flutter brilliantly, but do not fly.

We are locked into an intellectual feeding frenzy that gorges on the rigid teats of technology, and we have bought this wagon-load of mule dung that has us believing that we are surfing in the cool-blue of cyberspace and all that we are left with in the end is 'media-driven consciousness.'

Technological advancement has created an intellectual paradigm before which the private world of self-reflection sinks away. Science, despite its usefulness, does not appear to have created a **virtuality** out of which we can feel the strength of self-direction, nor is it a substance from which we can thrive emotionally. We are left yearning to return to days of simpler activities; to walk along the wide streets, our imaginations riding on the wind of a soft summer evening, children laughing and playing into the darkening safety of the twilight hours, the sound of their small feet running, distant voices drifting upward and the night air floating with the scent of honeysuckle and ambrosia . . . as though we could return . . . and we are left with the enormity of a task that will unlikely return us to these simpler days, to these harmless pleasures.

To turn back the hands of time and yet go forward, is a chore that dwarfs our spirit. We are left to the world of fugitive imaginings, only stolen dreams of surcease.

But can we really let go of our desire for innocent times? As Mary Renault so artfully phrased it in her book entitled 'Persian Boy'; "The sons of dreams long outlive the sons of seeds!"

Although this address on Tai Chi does not pretend to survey the entirety of human evolution, it can be more reasonably seen as an attempt to make the present social situation more identifiable and perceptible by throwing the reader a line of self-initiative; tying awareness, as it were, to the hook of self-reflection, which in turn will allow the truth-climber to feel more complete in the moment.

In the course of this reading, the student will be pointed toward a new attitude and may discover a comprehensible permanence through **self-possession;** and perhaps gain a more complete awareness through a creative dynamism found by way of enlarging the capacity for spontaneous self-expression. To achieve this elevated condition of consciousness the student must become engaged in the regulation of available biological energy.

This suggests the building of energy reserves through specific energy-conservation principles handed down through millennia. This points to the early pioneers of health who let us see the first traces of energetic-dynamics that flowed throughout the human body.

These workings can be seen, for example, in what is undeniably the oldest 'medical system' known to humankind, namely - *acupuncture.*

This system of understanding the activity flow of physical and mental energy is over four thousand years old and happens to be the brain-child of China.

Through this remarkable approach in health-maintenance we can clearly recognize the gift of genius left to us; indeed a legacy of wholeness that continues to be used for the good of humanity. We are left to proceed with greater awareness, all of us riding the wave of countless generations who have transformed the lifeblood of the past into the viability of the future.

Through Tai Chi's unique approach we can set a novel and potent standard for the appropriate use of personal energy.

Tai Chi is a process that is divided into three elements: there is an *active* phase, which is readily identifiable as 'dynamic movement.' This phase teaches the student how to access the flow of power that drives the human organism through the quantitative articulations as expressed in the Tai Chi form-play.

The second element is the *passive* phase, which allows the student to be more "observant," and to sense the character and quality of the physical dynamics and aesthetic movements. At the same time, the passive component is tied essentially to the quality of 'mindfulness' which is brought to the form, or posture, being **played** with during practice.

There is a third force to be considered, and that is the **neutral** phase which is not at all easily identifiable, but nevertheless acts as a fulcrum, so to speak, for the dynamic interchange between the active and passive phases. The neutral component rests on the capacity to **sense** the shift from the active to the passive in much the same way that the driver of a race-car throws the stick-shift into neutral before he shifts from first to second gear, and so on.

The angle of awareness related to the neutral phase is directed toward a mental alertness that senses the precise moment that activity must slow or speed up. This subtle component also acts to regulate energy output through extending power with efficient control.

Again, this phase can be seen as a quieting of displayed energy.

It is this special kind of attentive awareness placed on the triad of energy-dynamics that places Tai Chi in a rather unique class which harnesses physical power to mental control.

Through Tai Chi's aesthetic lessons in self-awareness we are given the opportunity to expand our capacity for greater mental focus and we are challenged to develop a new language for psychic and emotional content. The Tai Chi method of approach is an original and innovative plan that creates an artful space for self-examination and represents an advanced platform for the psycho-physiological exercises that come to be used for the production of 'high energy-substances,' in the form of encaphalons and endorphins.

We are literally seeding a new firmament for self-healing and self-rejuvenation with an emphasis on mental focus and self-awareness. Fundamentally, we are engaged in a focalizing process which can be transposed to the events that form our daily routine. Here is a foundation for learning how to intensify the experiences, events, the happenings and occurrences of our journey through life!

It is here within the philosophy of Tai Chi, that we can embrace, as it were, all that is perhaps unfamiliar, yet healthful, and we are empowered to move quietly toward a sense of truth that seems to rest just beyond our reach. Tai Chi leaves us to explore the boundaries of self-awareness and yet it apprehends a feeling of daring to be limitless. It encourages a seeking of relationship to everything while denying communication to nothing outside the bounds of human concern.

In truth, we seek to experience life in all its displays, but we require a sense of purposeful action and have need of establishing an anchor of self-affirmation which will fortify our personal capacities.

Through directing our awareness more to *self* and eliminating negative discussion about 'others,' we will be inspired to engage in the activities and interests which make up the *real* fabric of life, which after all is said and done, belongs to the grander outlook of cultural exchange. Our aim needs to be steadied and we must begin to enlarge our personal awareness if we seek to enhance our capacity to reach our full potential as human beings. We must expand our information-field and till the soil of new ground which is evidenced, and tendered, through the Tai Chi methodology.

Let us move beyond the spoon-fed approaches in self-development offered by the money-making machine of marketing-devices and become more familiar with the kind of energy we can develop through a personal 'self-signature', and become more intimately connected with the quest to understand the finer workings of the body and mind.

Are we nothing more than human-squirrels on pricey, cheerless treadmills, given carefully planned psychological/television-injections in the form of "info-mercials" which bind us to boring physical repetitions? How can we withstand this attack on our intelligence, and furtherstill, how do we endure this blatant assault on our personal sense of creative enterprise?

This is the carefully measured dose of commercial 'sodium pentathol' which has us responding with credit-card mentality, and we find ourselves behaving like somnambulists out for a walk to apparent freedom from "all our ills."

At best, the economic war waged by commercial and industrial mercenaries, is a body-politic that is schemingly imposed on the unwary consumer, and offers little more than a multiple choice menu of endless machines, which leave us empty of personal initiative!

Their well-established foothold points to society's concern with quick-fixes, which have to do with the conformity to 'image' and reveals the indifference toward the unique conditions of 'self'!

These dealings are the stuff from which grows mistrust and are taken from the larger list of human misconduct that paralyzes our confidence in humanity's quest for sincere inter-relatedness.

Let us do away with the costly and cumbersome contraptions which strip us of personal expression and rob us of our creative undertakings; appliances which in fact drive to reinforce our laxity and act to conjure emotional states of dullness.

These are some of the prime apprehensions and considerations that are embraced by a system of comprehension that evolved from the human need for well-being and for understanding our place in an otherwise unknown universe. This is the earth of Tai Chi; an antique pathway that reveals to us an approach in living that speaks of passionate enterprise, self-composure and personal order.

However unprepared we appear to be at this juncture in time, the rhythm of life can be found in the heart of global exchange. In contrariety, and rather than 'taking the tack' to familiarize us with the finer workings of humanitarian inter-relatedness, stands the modern communicating networks which have prematurely exposed us to the dark emotions of a negative microcosm, and with little regard for the ramifications on our emotional and psychological status.

There are many in the West who have been caught in the web of exotic, external appearances related to oriental culture and fail to appreciate the underlying elements of genuine human regard associated with the profound, yet pragmatic, approach in healthful living which is found through the cultivation of Tai Chi principles.

The cultural value in the study of Tai Chi lies in the way it trains the mind in logical thinking, in clarity of expression, and in keen insight into the meanings and sources of man's struggle with the forces of the world around him. This scholarly prize of China is a unique and multi-faceted approach in self-awareness and whole-person healthcare. Tai Chi can be seen as a bridge of agreement between the attitudes of the east and the west, fusing the framework of an age-old technology with the requirements of the individual, in an otherwise modern world.

Tai Chi's self-directed philosophical content opens a window to man's search for *meaning,* and herein lies the heart of the Tai Chi philosophy which is rooted in the profound attitudes and disciplines gathered with great sacrifice along the ancient route by the Chinese sages.

Their worthy sacrifices were made in an attempt to create a deeper understanding in human inter-relatedness and personal order; an order which stresses the relationship between an individual's health and the elements which compose their inner and outer environment.

The essential components shed light on individual psychological posture and those key elements which compose individual emotional content. On a physical level, choice of food and even proper times to harvest are part of this encompassing philosophy.

The components so far discussed are embraced by the theory of 'yin and yang,' one which offers us the preventative power for acquiring sound health and emotional well-being by moving beyond the mainly symptomatic approach of Western medicine.

As a health-care nation we must face the stark reality of society's increasingly powerless ability to cope with an impending avalanche of degenerative diseases now threatening to engulf the industrialized world.

The theory of the yin/yang approach takes all aspects of human development into consideration as in; the strengths and weaknesses of our genetic stamping; environmental conditions; eating habits; postural tension, and our activity level.

'Yin and yang' act in mutual accord and represent a polar-expression in the perpetual change that accompanies all human activity. That is to say, through the development of insight into the varied conditions which compose the lifestream of human experiences, there comes a growing sensitivity to the signs of a particular set of changes before they assume a larger and perhaps more threatening appearance.

In the simplest of terms, yin and yang points to the relationship of the various extremes in our nature and how these extremes produce symptoms of pain, confusion and discomfort. In more subtle terms, we sometimes come to learn that in the face of adversity and opposition, through which encounters we may very well be crushed, we are asked to reach for hidden strength, and paradoxically, these obstacles present us with an opportunity to overcome our doubts.

Moving to examples that are in keeping with more classical terms; any action which closes in upon itself, as is the case in depression, identifies the dominant force called 'yang.' This state may also be identified as one of contraction (yang); a pulling of energy into greater density and thereby a becoming 'heavier,' and can be seen as a movement toward the 'interior.'

The yang aspect is further exemplified in the phenomenology of physiological respiration as seen in the inspiration (inhaling) phase with the breath proceeding inward and filling the lungs with the density of oxygen.

Furthermore, the inhalation phase (yang) produces heat, and is aptly illustrated in the coiled strength of tension as evidenced when the diaphragm contracts.

On the other hand, referring to the expiration (exhalation) phase, the lungs empty (yin) and as the breath leaves the body it moves into the open (yin), proceeding as it were to the space (yin) of the exterior.

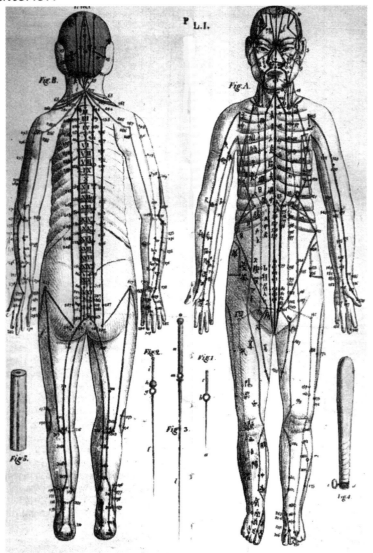

"Yin and Yang point to a relationship which suggests a pulse of interchangeable energy."

Yin is connected with expansion, and can further be interpolated as emotional exhilaration. This state of expansion is a developing outward; a centrifugal action which produces softness, lightness, and a change to coolness.

Yin and yang are not simply linear opposites, but remain interconnected, just as the lungs engage in a perpetual adjustment, first filling steadily, then emptying gradually, and the inter-relatedness never assumes the appearance of a static state.

Dusk and dawn are also prime examples of a 'relationship,' rather than a fixed disparity between dominating and supplicating forces. When the light of day gradually disappears and reveals the canopy of stars, it suggests a gradual and growing receptivity to darkness (yin); that is to say, an opening to the hidden realm of nightfall that has always existed behind the great light of the sun's activity (yang).

The typical Western interpretation sees yin and yang as opposites in division, or even in contention, rather than in complimentary interdependence.

Yin and yang point to a relationship, which in effect develops all matters and energies toward a state of balance, and essentially reveals the signs of necessary change.

Again, this is not a stagnant portrait and is not simply a pointing to the obverse, then the reverse of the same coin! It is the whole coin itself, which is identified through seeing that the 'heads' is distinguished by its *relationship* to the 'tails' and vice versa.

It suggests a pulse of interchangeable energy, as witnessed in the ebb and flow of the tides, with their inward and outward movements. Indeed, it is aptly found in the ascent and descent of the ocean's motion, as much as it is detected in the pattern of atomic particles which fold inward to the proton and unfold outward to the electron.

Space (void) is considered yin, and time (form) is considered yang, and respectively so are those human activities which are either psychological (yin), or physical (yang). In this way we can see that yin and yang express a distinct and inseparable duality, a 'copulation' of sorts, that ultimately reveals a virtual unity.

The key to the affinity between yin and yang is called **shiang sheng**, that is - mutual ascension or inseparability. The conception of a bird in flight immediately brings to mind the image of air; and so does water come to life when we imagine a fish swimming about. Take the words of Lao-Tsu as translated by Gia-fu Feng:

> *Thirty spokes unite at the wheel's hub*
> *It is the center hole that makes it useful*
>
> *Shape clay into a vessel*
> *It is the space within that makes it useful*
>
> *Cut out doors and windows for a room;*
> *It is the holes which make it useful*
>
> *Therefore profit comes from what is there*
> *Usefulness from what is not there*

Thus the parts vitally serve in the construction of an expanded whole. There is no separation, no razor-line dividing these qualities of existence, but rather a demonstration of co-existence and of mutual reception. The scope of factors conserve and promote one another in building up the entire form.

It is here that we arrive at a **union** in which one yin and one yang form what is called the Tao.

The same bipolar picture appears when considering body-weight as we keep in mind that body weight *changes* and develops gradually whether toward a 'lighter' (yin) weight, or a 'heavier' (yang) state.

Temperature is also a dynamic state of yin and yang, cold or hot, dry or wet, and not merely the temperature which suits us when on holiday.

Inclusively, yin and yang point to sexual inter-relatedness which identifies female (yin) and male (yang), as well as to the spectrum of colors as when light is reduced to a polarity in color: purple/yellow - blue/orange - green/red - black /white; and beyond to the human attitudes of gentleness/aggression, and repose/activity, all of which are respectively "yin and yang."

Even the organs themselves are classified into yin and yang which is however not the course of study in this book, but can be referenced through Chinese traditional medicine and acupuncture, which refer to the condition of 'chi,' in quality and texture, that is found in the organs respectively. And that, is the yin and yang of it!

The tools for discovering the secret to the intensification of conscious life, to good health and well-being, are found in the dynamic relationship of yin and yang which extends from the aspect of physical dynamics to an awakening of consciousness so as to open the doors of perception.

What ensues is a new order in thinking and planning, and a distinct mode of being is discovered which presents the student of Tai Chi with a new attitude in relation to time and space.

Time is no longer the yardstick for work, while *expectation* represents an unfavorable attitude that drags upon the coat-tails of labor. The 'work' should be done for its own sake - for its own sacredness! The transitory and fragile moments can then be brought to life more brilliantly, richer in rhythm, in variation, and actual experience. All begins to move with *alacrity* rather than with mechanical movements that are clothed in rigidity, and which stand in relation to 'fixed' time and is decreed by the relentless dictates of success and failure.

Reality is a changing, dynamic interplay of events that allows yesterday to coincide with tomorrow. This is not so much "philosophy," but rather a mode of awareness which introduces a new approach in perceiving the patterns of life that come into our experience. All this comes about through an evolution which proceeds toward a novel pattern in thinking, or perhaps it might better be said - 'musing.'

When was the last time you sat in front of a fireplace on a cold wintry night and watched the golden and red flames flicker and dance, and listened to the crack and hiss of the wood? Perhaps you fell asleep and later awoke to see the last crimson embers breathing their final colors.

When was the last time you lay in an open field on a balmy summer eve and watched the sun turn into a ghostly orange ball and slip behind the charcoal trees? This is not so much thinking but rather *reflection*.

Here is the kernel of contemplation and the seed of meditation which brings us from a dimension to the dimensionless. In contrast, thinking is the seed of explanation and serves our capacity to construct a dimension.

The common attitude in thinking about 'things' is to consider the usefulness of the thing. That seems fair at first glance, but it falls short of entire reality!

The yin/yang replaces the utilitarian approach by introducing a meditative induction based on "cause and effect."

For example, take your perception of an apple; "This red fruit smells good - tastes sweet - and it's good for me!" All that may be true, but it is only a slice of reality. Leaving off from this commonplace response, we may also venture on to the old argument of which came first, the apple seed or the apple tree?

In a Taoist sense the "meditation" may proceed thusly; "The apple seed drifted windborn - buried itself in earth - grew through many years in a relationship to the atmosphere, birds, insects, and human beings - reached maturity, and apple blossoms bloomed - the smallest buds appeared and thereafter the green round fruit came into being - the apple *transformed* through its own maturation and presented itself, red and sweet, to the world around it."

Although this deductive, or meditative level of perception may well be taken for granted, it is representational and demonstrates that life does not stand still, nor does it remain at the same point in time. Life does not endure in the same form, nor does it continue in the same appearance, nor does it prevail with the same quality of being.

Life is a flux, a 'shape-shifting,' very much dependent on endogenous elements and factors and influenced by exogenous components and materials.

The state of consciousness found in the 'mind-set' of Tai Chi involves *time* as a background for change and for seeing life as a continuum starting from yin, considered **passive**, that is 'in-waiting'; just as the apple blossom passively remains in-waiting for the flying insect to carry its pollen and to further assist in the birth of new life. The change is gradual as the insect firstly **asserts** itself in the yang mode and carries on from flower to flower, both receiving (yin) and giving (yang) in an exchange that will bring abundance both to itself, to the community of insects to which it belongs, to the tree, and even to man.

This balance demonstrates the yin and yang of existence and illustrates the mutual reliance on **another**, hence identifying the harmonious link that joins all aspects of life.

In the human arena, what needs to be considered is a keener perception of 'process,' which implies that what is most desirable is developing an awareness that can delve into the subtle transformations that identify the **essence of reality**, which will bring a greater appreciation of the relation between cause and effect.

In this regard, and returning to our earlier analogy, not only is it insightful to say: "The apple doesn't fall far from the tree!," It is also fair to exclaim, "The apple is the essence of the tree!"

Although the tree and the apple are far from similar, there is no doubt in our minds that one has developed **from** the other!

Indeed, they are as different as 'my eye' compared to 'my hand,' but both come from the 'same' human body and none other!"

It is in the 'invisibility of transformation' that we begin to see what we don't see, and perhaps in our study of Tai Chi and its main tenet, expressed as yin and yang, we will have cause to better appreciate the relationship of 'cause and effect.'

What can be more readily approached is that an inescapable dualism bisects nature, so that each entity is a half, each thing is the object of its own subject, and each thing suggests another thing to make it whole; just as two magnets repel and attract each the other, by virtue of their polarity.

It is as though each magnet was looking to complete itself by either accepting or rejecting.

Perhaps this striving takes place in a way that we cannot understand, but yet there is a palpable drive to bring the forces of which the magnet is made up into equilibrium.

This balance extends just as well in the human world, for it is that every delight has a commensurate penalty set on its abuse!

Every defect prompts an excess, just as every excess brings about a defect, as is the case for simple sugar-cane which becomes a harbinger of destruction when left to become rum.

The glutton will answer to moderation with his life!

So it seems that for every achievement there is a failure, and for every thing you gain there is something you lose.

The cup must be empty in order that it be full!

The gist of the universe negotiates itself into every corner. If the pure is there, so is the tainted; if the kinship, so the enmity; if the force, so the hindrance; a consummate fidelity calculates its balance in all parts of life. Every secret told - every lie unfolds - every trespass halted - every decency rewarded. Crime and punishment grow on the same branch.

Life is categorically empowered with inescapable circumstances which the foolish seek to avert. Some escape the situation in one way only to be set upon by another set of controlling factors.

The wild stag in Aesop's fable revered his horns and denounced his cloven-hooves, but when the hunter gave chase, his feet delivered him from danger, and later, snared in the brush, his horns destroyed him.

A chain is only as strong as its weakest link. Our strength grows out of our weakness!

"Life is empowered with inescapable circumstances which the foolish seek to avert."

Cheapest is dearest. Without effort there is no achievement. Nothing ventured, nothing gained!

When shoved aside, pushed into submission, distraught and crushed under the weight of unexpected circumstance, we have an opportunity to discover a deeper truth. What we accrue is new evidence - our naïveté corrected - our bragging cured.

What we earn is appreciation. What we acquire is insight. What we procure is capacity. Under all these stars that perch with perfect balance, lies the original source of being.

Being is the boundless confirming of life, self-balanced and embracing all connections unto itself.

Man's life is more a *process* and not so much a product! But to us in our deviated state - procrastinating, listless, reluctant, with our machines advancing, but not our souls - out of harmony with natural laws - outside the affairs of divine expansion - the evolvement comes in waves of trauma!

We are not convinced of the wealth of the soul in its eternal beauty and ubiquity. We do not accept the goings on of today, nor can we believe that any of them can emulate or re-animate the wondrous experiences of yesterday.

The yin and yang of it is a process in reeducating, if not transfiguring our awareness so that life can be seen in its wholeness, and subsequently man can begin to live closer to nature and once more embrace the truth of self-reality, which has more to do with appreciating the interconnectedness of things, acknowledging change, and more wisely accepting the inevitable process of transformation.

There is also something to be said about being far less concerned with our aberrated need to control inert matter, or the curious attempts to alter the patterns of time and space. The effort to control nature is after all an artificial stranglehold on evolution.

If we were more concerned with the "essence of our being" rather than with the "substance of our image," life would take on new meaning, and the aura of truth would better allow us to appreciate the mine of wisdom that lies at the heart of man's awareness.

In a broader sense, yin and yang reflect the progress of Mankind in its struggle for human and social inter-relatedness, and then again it represents the battle of the individual in his rise from the ego-centered puppet to the cosmic-oriented soul. Yin and Yang are the systole and diastole of the Tai Chi heart and involve every aspect of man's behavior, and can be applied to the instinctive, motor, emotional and intellectual centers.

This creative work moves with clarity to a point beyond the wearing of 'masks,' which is a terribly weak compensation for the requirements of human intimacy. We can only watch how awkwardly the individual 'dances' through life, and whose curious movements only reflect the half-hearted strategies used to acquire honor, love and power. Here is the latticework of imagined reality and is certainly not the clearest way to **awakening**.

Tai Chi calls upon the individual to rally to the needs of consciousness and conclude that man's **ordinary** state of consciousness, his so called 'waking state,' is not the highest level of awareness of which he is capable! It was G. Gurdjieff who spoke with words that ring with imposing clarity when he called consciousness a "waking sleep."

"*Tai Chi represents the battle of the individual in his rise from the ego-centered puppet to the cosmic-oriented soul.*"

Tai Chi is an offering of artful knowledge that will help awaken the student to an augmented realm of **being**, placing the individual in a more effective position in relation to the affairs of the world. It creates a pathway permitting the individual to strike the inner chord of self-reality so that it rings true with the higher octave of creative enterprise.

Underway is a transformational process which directs our energy through new corridors of experience; beyond our emotional frustrations that are caught up in the anxieties of earning a living, and past the accumulated material possessions that are used to fill the spiritual void of our lives. In this new place of self-elevation we stand outside the feeling of doom that is associated with mass-producing systems that batter our senses into dull passivity.

In the Tai Chi sanctuary we reach into a private, personal interiority, an especially contemplative relationship that slips into the realm of fugitive wanderings and unique secret spaces. In the beginning our transportations linger, but their brevity only makes the experience all the more precious. We slide into worlds of Sung scrolls that are filled with images of fields and mountains and see ourselves in the great distance sitting calmly beneath a flowering tree. We step onto the field of infinite reflection and wrap ourselves in nesting layers of stillness and serenity.

We have arrived at the door of creative multiplicity and through this "introspection" we are inspired to reach beyond the vulgarizing effects of a materially prosperous, but inwardly impoverished society.

For the most part, as it stands, our attitudes are ensnared in cultural tokens and voguing, and we need to impose a new attitude upon ourselves so as to move beyond the repressiveness of our overly casual handling of experience.

With this thought in mind, let us open our eyes and study just a few of the outlandish rituals and practices of affluent society that weighs the importance of the last years of life on striking a 'little white ball' through the air into a small dark hole! This preoccupation is after all a game of status quo which proceeds on shambling steps across an open field of manicured grass in dismal pursuit of a dimpled piece of tightly rolled elastic.

At the other end of the city others are found to be sitting in chairs for hours at a time in an almost comatose state, with their heads in a heated-helmet that will set the 'coif' for the weekend.

In the last years of life there are those who prefer to be judiciously assaulted by dough-like kneading in hope of bringing back lost biological vigor, and then again there are some who will reduce their existence to bludgeoning their bodies and faces with surgical procedures so as to insure a meager few years of extended vanity at the cost of aggravating the dangers of disfigurement.

This is the sentence of self-aggrandizement that awaits the honorable members of society which would somehow remind them that their lives were not spent uselessly.

How different would the history be of one who could carry past the plethora of overstated dogmas and the white-haired abracadabra of religions in *articulo mortis*. How different it would be for the individual who could step beyond 'consumptive urgency' and no longer submit to the power of disingenuous commercial ideologies that foster conspicuous consumption and are armed with the unique and cruel talent of exacerbating greed for 'lares and penates.'

Imagine how it would feel to be protected from the shortsightedness of a thin education that crams the cerebral brain full of facts and figures, while giving lip-service to the physical body by encouraging dangerous, competitive sports; and then, with 'intellectual suitcase' in hand, discharges countless individuals into the concrete jungle, neither having prepared them for human intimacy, nor ready for self-comprehension.

"We live in a spiritually impoverished culture that is profuse with lickspittle, tufthunting, and social sycophancy."

At best, this 'canned version' of social education is a hammering of the heart against the anvil of conformity and a forging of the soul into a mechanical condition of inward bankruptcy. And finally, it is a throwing of the individual into a spiritually impoverished culture that is profuse with lickspittle, tufthunting, and self-serving sycophancy.

The knowledge, encapsulated in the Tai Chi approach, although thousands of years aged, may very well be a 'balm' for a society that has placed material concerns, social backslapping, and technological stratagems, far too forward of the need for self-awareness.

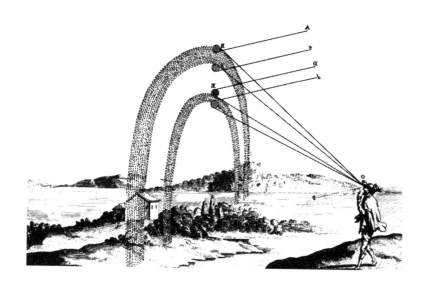

"There was a time when 'seekers of reality' searched for the masterwork of truth."

Detour from Reality

*"Only to a magician is the world
forever fluid, infinitely mutable
and eternally new. Only he knows
the secret of Change, only he knows
truly that all things are crouched in
eagerness to become something else,
and it is from this universal tension
that he draws his power."*

— Peter Beagle

There was a time when 'seekers of reality' searched for the masterwork of truth; for direction and comfort which they could not find in the plain world of land and law.

On the great windswept plateau of endless time the voices of antiquity are muted by the glare of the white silence of the modern city. There are those who are resigned to living on the periphery and are limited to vicarious gleanings taken from the realm of social order; an order which offers a fragmented view of reality.

After all, we the living, dare not wander beyond some small discomfort and have managed our lives on symbols; we the survivors, who have been left to rummage through the sparse clippings of exaggerated metaphors which stand as ultimate truths that leave us as empty as the space around us.

The knowledge left behind probes into the depths of an alarming realization; we know nothing more about the human soul than did our ancestors who meandered through the hazy heat of existence and faced the falling sands of time.

Then again there were the rare ones, those remarkable few who struggled with the puzzle of life, with the pieces of evolution, and with the elusive meaning of private and universal reality.

Despite the ancients, in their wise ingressions, and in a virtual sense, we are left only with symbols and we have grown to rely on half-hearted gestures and elaborate rituals so as not to suffer our colossal ignorance. We have inherited the relics, ciphers, cryptograms, hieroglyphs and ideograms of 'long-lost awareness' and we are left in the shadows of a milliard of self-serving icons that have been carefully dusted in the muted museums of Mankind's folly. It is not that we don't care! In fact, we desperately want to know, to come to grips with perhaps what is the inarguable truth of our beginnings, but we are resigned to the thinness of artifacts and stratagems which leave us dangling on the edge-of-never-knowing.

On the rim of time, falling like a falling star, the world we call Earth spins ever so slowly, so wistfully, steadily hovering along an invisible track of secret design. Majestically holding true to her course, this ocean-planet rides the ancient cosmic currents, and on her surface creatures of every kind and beings of every dimension remain indifferent to her streaming speed through incalculable space.

"Holding true to her course, this ocean-planet rides the ancient cosmic currents."

Time paints her pictures on the living creatures who crowd together on a small swirling-ship named Earth; some who will romp briefly on her weathered shores and others who gambol along her mountain paths. There are those who skim and glide beneath her undulating surface, and still others who ride atop sea-beaten vessels that crawl across her glistening body. The mysterious rays of distant stars converge on them, breathing life into their ever-changing forms, and altogether the magical elements of natural forces have clothed each living thing separately.

From beyond, the grouping of magnificent suns are moving points of light who shed their pristine heat into the icy ignorance of boundless space. Man stares upward at a single eye of glowing brilliance, stunned by the vast and living presence of a fierce and fiery globe; a lone star that maintains an invincible attitude that grants man power and life. Curiously, and with great ingenuity, man has come to imitate the power of this great orb so as to furnish his cities with light and fuel his homes with heat. Below, we walk along the littered beaches with growing awareness of the soiled seas, and we stare abstractly into an open hole of atmosphere that pulls our ineffectual thoughts into the incomprehensible future.

Here we are, altogether, spinning silently through the starry haze of the endless aerosphere, unable to perceive the fathomless reality of existence, while the tides of infinity have long been upon us as they blow their invisible lessons through the valleys of a world that is only beginning to recognize the awesome ecological reality of an "interconnected universe."

All this happens in the hour-glass of time and passes through countless epochs in the dreamy geometry of human reason.

Man views the infinite quality of birth and death and witnesses the hidden dialogue of evolutionary transformation. He plainly sees that life is forever changing; like liquid time that shapes itself with every breath. He has grown to understand that the substance of life cannot be completely mastered despite the ingenuity of his contrivances. In the great pool of inventions, his fingers send ripples to future generations and from the tension of his genius and the clutching-hand of greed, he sees the reflection of Man the legend. He is trapped in the twilight dimension of boundless space and his body is living proof of a stupendous miracle that holds the richness of his private memories that are left in the diary of unspoken feelings.

With mind and body, he is left to find the long-way home as he searches in quiet desperation along a mysterious pathway that moves from the abandoned to the anticipated, from the arena of inner defeat to the theater of outer triumphs, and from the river of uncertainty to the sea of courage. For now, he sets the mainsails for lost time and heads along a route beyond retracing. The winds of nostalgia are too weak to change his course, but still he glances back to see the wake of vanished days.

There is an accepted, universal belief that we are driving forward toward a higher octave in evolution, and indeed we have progressed intellectually. Yet there is something off in our capacity to make sense of it all!

It is with bold and rapid strokes that over the last generation we have produced such a large volume of information, which by its very immensity, we are left to struggle in an attempt to use it properly.

We are witnessing how modern civilization is degenerating into the abyss of fascination with the sciences of inert matter, and the enchantment moves with specious steps that overshadow our capacity to stay in stride.

Man has been brazen in his attitude and belief that there is little cost to his emotional and psychological status when he transgresses the laws of natural order.

We must be wary of our thrusts into what has become an uncertain future and perhaps it is in our interest to reexamine the meaning of **progress**.

The image of progress is modern in its version of a utopian society and was cast wholly in Western European culture. As a result of the work of Sir Issac Newton, in the 17th century, new evidence came forward that revealed the universe to be governed by immutable laws that had been in operation since the start of creation and would persist to operate into the undying future. In this sense progress took on an altogether new meaning which saw man's evolution as perfectible due to the immeasurable and indefinite amount of time stretching into the beyond, giving the human race ample opportunity to work out its destiny.

As far back as 1791, Alexander Hamilton concluded, in his **Report on Manufacturers** prepared for the Congress, that progress was intimately connected to the marriage of industrial and technological advances which in turn granted economic prosperity. Hamilton asserted that not only affluence, but also the sovereignty and the security of the country, depended upon the wealth and exploits of manufacturers. He went on to say that industrial advance was necessary for the perfection of our political institutions and that industry intrinsically supported the safety and welfare of the entire society.

In the 1830's the **Sadler Report** awoke Parliament to the deplorable conditions connected to technological advance.

We have only to look at the events of working conditions during the Industrial Revolution to understand the wake of human degradation and the inhumane practices associated with technology and industrialism.

Technology was epitomized by the 'Machine' which was nefarious in dehumanizing man and preyed upon society's groveling preference for material requirements over spiritual imperative.

On Dec. 6, 1852, President Millard Fillmore delivered his third annual address and offered appreciable insight into the dangers of innovation; "It is not strange . . . that such an exuberance of enterprise should cause some individuals to mistake change for progress."

During the mid nineteenth century we witnessed a systematic correspondence of the scientific and engineering communities. But by the end of the nineteenth century many intellectuals had recoiled from the idea of progress.

Leo Tolstoy viewed the direction in which science and technology were proceeding as pernicious to man's true nature.

Henry Adams believed that industrial society was strangling the imaginative resourcefulness of man - that his creativity, love, and his aesthetic intuitions, which were responsible for the creation of such masterworks as the Sistine chapel and the cathedrals of Mont St. Michel and Chartres, were being shattered.

We are faced with a similar dilemma engaging the eco-conscious individual today, and many more of us, with each short decade, are witnessing the growing merger of science and technology, along with associated research and development.

The pledge to educational criteria has dramatically increased with new emphasis on upbeat teaching programs which favor inter-connecting the scientific, economic and managerial techniques of innovation. We watch the big-wheel of technology turn and where it stops nobody knows, but one thing is certain, individual inventiveness has become, for the most part, a charade in the quest for self-aggrandizement and man has become a slave to material glory.

Scientific insight and the achievements of technology appear to be the seal of progress. A steady growth in the measure of the gross national product in tandem with a low unemployment rate are taken to be the corresponding indicators of national development.

Yet progress has its price when many cannot even begin to compete in an overcrowded market-place because they do not have the capital to exploit the new technology, thereby leaving the "kill" to the multinational corporations who have easy access to the natural resources and are able to deploy the market strategies necessary for arguable success.

We can see that progress is a peculiar, Janus-faced value system that impeaches the 'little man' as he attempts to rub shoulders with the giants who are clearly bent on stifling the entire meaning of free enterprise.

There was a time when the formula for progress was tied into three important factors; savings, investment, and increases in labor productivity, all of which were regarded as prime conditions influencing economic prosperity. Our present state of affairs is dictated by the revolutionary criteria stemming from technological innovation. Yet, to assure continued progress, it is necessary to have properly trained and knowledgeable people, as well as a burgeoning market to consume the superflux of new-sprung artifacts streaming out of this modern cornucopia.

Those in positions of authority and power charge to exploitation and success, which permits them to disregard the human entanglements of their determinations.

In a 1963 publication entitled, *The Role of Science in Civilization*, published by Harper and Row, one could read Robert B. Lindsay's wave-of-the-hand comment which provides a striking example of rationalization and justification for *progress* as follows; " . . . mankind has to pay a price for the joy of a more exciting if more dangerous life provided by technology."

In the March issue of *Science* in 1967, many avid readers attended this viewpoint from the President of the National Academy of Sciences, Philip Handler, who offered the following attitude in regards to progress; " For most of us gathered here, it is an article of faith that the attainment of an ever more complete and penetrating understanding of man and the universe in which he finds himself is, of itself, one of mankind's highest goals . . . the knowledge [science] so gained will be translated into the technology which, tomorrow, will serve as the means by which man will raise himself from his animal estate, loosen him from his inherent biological limitations, and thus free him for whatever spiritual goals lie ahead."

Handler placed great importance on the perfectibility of man, however not through moral edification, or sentiments of love, fidelity, and compassion, but through technology and scientific instruction. Further entries disclosing the maze-like impunities of our social and material progress would be superfluous and these examples are sufficient in explaining our civilized 'ride to Utopia.'

As it is, modern civilization has been assembled without any regard for natural cadences, nor with the concern for organic limits.

Man assumes that his audacious activities will flourish without self-punishment.

Science's runaway child, whose name is Technology, has provided unbridled power to the industrial and commercial production-machines which have weighed us down with idle curiosities. Individual aspirations and theories belonging to scientific appetites have created the circumstances and events of social normalcy, and have in all seriousness, attempted to define the totality of a human being.

Indeed, beneath the veil of scientific secrecy are systems of investigation that aspire to explain man in his entirety. In effect the parts are seen as the whole!

The cases in point follow thusly; from the concreted view of skeletal evolution, man's physical self is seen through the eyes of anthropology; through psychology, he is viewed by definition of the mental, or "inner aspect" of his being; through communal events he is the study of sociology.

Man cannot be unified, never made whole!

He is, after all, an empirical subject who has been divided up according to the method of research employed. And here we sit in the halls of learning being asked to place our faith in the 'knowledge' that merely *identifies*!

Man is after all, simply a fact of contemporaneous familiarity that is plainly and precariously balanced on the thin finger of *revealed* reality.

In effect, Science is guided by chance and by the directions of curiosity that are preserved in tradition. There is scant concern for the consequences and ramifications of experimental inquisitiveness which has ironically and ultimately revolutionized world order and has given us an incomplete, if not false picture of reality.

What we have been left with are essentially *suggestions* that are claimed as sources of truth.

We cannot manipulate our environment by whim and fancy, nor can we allow our natural conditions to be controlled by the casual investigations and circumstances of a scientist's career. These men of letters, these myopic scholars, for the most part have no real insight into the role they play, nor can they perceive the ramifications of their own activity. Yet, they continue on in their ultimately futile knowledge, aspiring to grasp the nature of *being* itself.

Human evolution has been, for the most part, a colossal adventure in ego-centricity and modern man has been made to live as a foreigner in a world that he has erected.

Despite all the satisfaction that Science has provided and continues to supply, and in as much as we appear to have reached the summit of mechanical and technological brilliance, this experimental body of knowledge that has merged so well with technology, has imposed its own sardonic time-table on our activities and has unwittingly managed to separate us even further from the universe, which after all, is our home.

The substance of our lives, more and more, is being gathered from the warehouse of synthetic emotions provided cheaply by the realtors of hyper-reality. We find ourselves enslaved by artificial devices that sequester our capacity for emotional inter-relatedness. We are left to cybernetic performances and computerized maneuvers in the cool-blue of hyper-space that have taken the place of genuine creative and emotional expression.

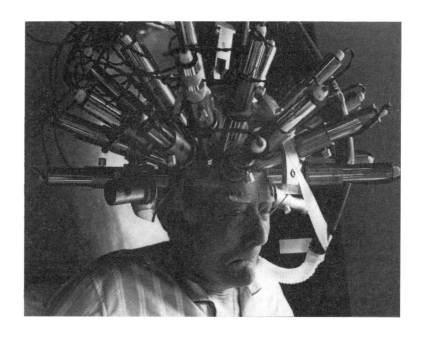

"We find ourselves enslaved by artificial devices that sequester our capacity for emotional inter-relatedness."

Let us always remember that Science was invented by Man, and Science is therefore human!

The events and circumstances of human evolution have crossed the paths of artists, poets, scientists and philosophers, each given to his own devices.

Man has sailed across the milky seas of the exosphere and plunged into the subworld of the microorganism, yet ironically, he has still to develop the wisdom of shaping his own inner life.

We feel the urge to know, not merely to speculate or dream. We live with the need to understand ourselves and transcend the inclemencies of modern life that threaten further emotional growth with entropic malice. Despite modern advances in science and technology, the human condition continues to slide into the arena of destitution. We have discovered prejudicial rents in the canopy of the human mind, and the light that has broken through reveals a parochial attitude that we can no longer afford to ignore.

In another sense, the world has also grown smaller, as technology has afforded us a more intimate look at the cultural and political elements which make up world communities. We are also being brought closer to a world-wide commonality that is struggling, albeit in the early stages, to develop a multi-fiber cultural thread-of-reason. That is to say, we are in the learning-field of global integration, in a sharing of history which will ultimately enrich our experience in living and perhaps settle our doubts about the unfamiliar and less readable activities and concerns of our fellow world-citizens.

Although there appears to be a malignant climate that is replete with cultural division, concurrently our modern era rings with growing voices that have begun to echo a moving desire to break out of our ethnocentric myopia. We are at a crossroads in coming to terms with the prospect of genuine cultural exchange!

The direction for humankind has been drawn on the great map of the technological future, while past attainments have been discarded in the wastebin of history, and the present has been assembled and reassembled from the glamorous gleanings of scientific adventurism. It is with certainty that the consequences of technological discoveries have revolutionized the world and made our civilization what it is.

In the course of centuries Man has devoured the earth itself!

The machine age has dried up the seas of oil. Industry has consumed the heartlands of coal. The atomic age has plundered our planet of the rare elements; cobalt, uranium, plutonium, leaving behind dangerous and worthless deposits of radioactive ashes and lead.

Yes, the scientific achievements of humanity are further developed than our intellectual and emotional powers.

We have leaped from vacuum tube to transistor, and beyond to the microchip. The various scientific communities, past and present, have stampeded toward nuclear fission, the hydrogen and atom bombs, and colossal energies have been acquired. Ironically, it appears that the peaceful use of atomic energies foretells the progress of world societies. It is not to abandon these powers, but to recognize that our emotional and mental status has manufactured a false sense of security and a distorted state of superiority, and rather than spending ourselves in further attempts to manipulate these arcane force-fields, it is more in our interest to gain control over the *inner-world* of our being.

Certainly the onslaught of scientific venturings has altogether changed the landscape of the twentieth century, but it has not changed the way we understand ourselves.

To many, especially in the West, and to world citizens who form the global community, people have come to see that increasing affluence, afforded by science and technology, has been accompanied by a growing lack of meaning in their personal lives. Indeed, a greatly improved standard of living does not of itself bring happiness or fulfillment and this realization has brought about a disenchantment with scientific and technical adventurism, and a yearning for a new dimension in experience which will help them regain a sense of direction.

Somewhere in the hourglass of time, there may very well lie a solution to a safer environment and to a more productive and peaceful world. But the glory of an answer remains obscured by our obsession with winning and competition. We have been seduced by the outer appearance of goals and attainment. We have grossly interfered with our natural rhythm, our natural self-hood, and have grown in such ways as to be denied the peace and well-being that would lift us from these neoteric imbalances. The instability of modern life, the ceaseless agitation, creates states of consciousness which bring about various nervous and organic disorders.

We have created our own dilemmas!

We have brought upon ourselves the various stresses and pathologies which threaten not only individual health and well-being, but also, our misdirected attitudes and misaligned ventures have grossly impacted the progeny of world societies.

At this time, solutions to these stifling inaccuracies and inconsistencies seem to lie beyond human hands, but not necessarily, outside the human mind.

There is but one instrument in Mankind's possession that can begin to untie the Gordian knot of ignorance and solve the mystery of our purpose for being here amongst the stars and spheres which reach beyond our perceptions, and perhaps discover, once and for all, our rightful place in an otherwise overwhelming universe.

The deciphering tool is the mind!

While the paths of the brain are plainly visible, the source of consciousness remains obscure. There are those who wish to tread the unexplored passages in the hope of finding the ultimate key which will unlock human reason and free man's wisdom, and open the door to the individual's 'true' identity. There are some who wish to unmask those secrets others have left behind and discover our final destination.

Whatever the case, there is a mental journey which of necessity must be taken through the arcane labyrinth of the mind, if we are to understand the significance of human evolution and the meaning of self-identity. To penetrate the inner recesses of the human mind is the "ultimate" excursion, and to devote ourselves, our lives, our energies to going further is the 'real' journey. Each step we take may be as uncertain as the last, yet each step will take us closer to the ultimate design which will see us reaching the summit of human compassion and have us soaring to the peak of creative intelligence. Whatever barricades we may encounter, we must prepare ourselves for the future by charting an intelligible course today.

In Man's journey toward self-realization he must surely conquer his doubts!

It is only then that he may expect to venture to the outer limits of his hopes and dreams. Each probative and measured step will find him coming closer to the ultimate truth, whose boundaries and frontiers are as yet unmapped. With each experience, self-confidence will be gained as he repeatedly overcomes doubt!

"To devote ourselves, our lives, our energies to going further, is the real journey."

In order to supplant the irresolute wanderings, in his search for self-reality, man's primary concern must be his standard of values and his choice of information. It is here that human beings have shown their greatest strength, and in the same breath, their monumental weakness.

Paradoxically, Man's endless search for knowledge has too often robbed him of his courage, for he has been seen to embrace the unknown with fear and suspicion rather than with open curiosity and wonder. He has reached into the depthless vault of his mind with grinding teeth rather than with reverence!

Nevertheless, of all the gifts given to man, perhaps the most precious is his mind, and with this abstract instrument of unknown design, he struggles untiringly to uncover the purpose and meaning of his life. He is caught in the classical struggle to differentiate what he is as a 'being' and what he makes of himself by 'becoming.'

Man is a fusion of polarities, and demonstrates, in all he says and does, a stream of contradictions, voids, and reversals. In his often unadmitted confusion, he uses **reason** as a drive to shelter himself within all that is conceivable. We probe the shoreless stretch of mind, seeking an answer as to our beginnings and whether we will find the way home to our heart.

But if an answer comes - will we hear? - will we understand? - will we approve?

Transcendental Stop

*"Flow with the tides of change and let
your mind be free of expectation.
Stay within yourself by honoring
your rightful place in life."*

— Chuang Tsu

Along the wide frontier of geological time, Man's journey is like a racing meteor that leaves a tiny but noticeable impression on the Earth's old face.

There is that sense in each of us that there is something missing from our lives. It is something intangible that hauntingly reminds us of how little time we have to find that missing piece which will determine the purpose and meaning of our lives.

We watch how the old world of forests and valleys have surrendered to the highways of modern routes, and instead of the perfume smells of exotic plants and aromatic greenery, the air is suffocated with the foulness of burning oil and gas.

In a world-wide sense there is only a dim awareness of how our management of space has changed our sense of time and reality, and in how many ways our modern efficiency has poisoned our sense of grace. It is in nature's stunning mirror that we can view man's crude attempt to stay in stride with fundamental universal order.

"Man's journey is like a racing meteor that leaves a tiny, but noticeable impression on the Earth's old face."

Nature proceeds from the dark background of the infinite. Her lessons can be seen, as exemplified through the remarkable provision of cell division, as can be seen in human growth and development, which carries on as microscopic entities appearing and attaching themselves in such a way so as to grow into a whole being through a succession of embryonic stages seen as, fish - amphibian - reptile - bird - and finally mammal.

This evolutionary pattern is immediate and takes place within the secret laboratory of the human organism. This developmental hierarchy, in order and kind, repeats itself in an evolutionary choreography, so to speak, and the unborn child duplicates, in successive transmutations, the forms of life belonging to those creatures that are born of the sea, air and land.

Once consolidated, the 'waiting' infant, as it were, swims in a saline sea of amniotic fluid, not unlike the ocean itself whose salt is verily in the entity's blood.

The initial pattern of development is a **transmutation** that progresses through a series of evolving models. The procession may be viewed as a whirling-dervish-like-spin, commencing with characteristics belonging to the denizens of the sea, as the early signs are marked by the breath pulsations of a fish's gills, then comes a cellular whirl that causes the **entity** to turn with the tail of a lizard, another whirl and comes now a "paddling" with the webbed digits of a swan; all encased in the enchanted lacework of creation - all responding to the polyphony of evolutionary magic.

So is the nature of the entity's progress as witnessed through the esoteric transitions in a transmigration of seemingly infinite amoeboids, spinning and somersaulting in a kind of chemical web, bringing with them meaningful messages from the odd fabric of genetic artistry.

Individually, these life-forms clamber for universal position and self-expression; these magical shreds of a soon-to-be-life, that come from creatures of remarkably different dimensions that pass through each other's lives like apparitions wending through doors in the house of the human body; they make their brief appearance, like ghosts hoping to reincarnate.

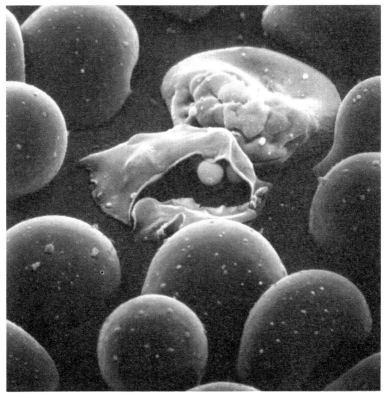

"Ten thousand things spring from the One!"
-*Tao Teh Ching*

In actuality, each entity begins as a single microorganism and transmogrifies to become a link in the chain of living creatures that are united in an organic ecosystem, which after all, has evolved from the same, albeit, recondite origin. When our knowledge becomes more complete we will discover that all things are the differentiation of one infinity. As Lao-Tsu succinctly pointed out long before the advent of biochemistry and recorded, as it is, in the 'Tao Teh Ching': "Ten thousand things spring from the One!"

This classical approach in Chinese philosophy has filtered its esoterica into the modern world and one of its "tributaries" has flowed into a pragmatic body of knowledge, having lengthened its reach through the dynamics of the "Tai Chi" approach.

Under consideration is the "underlying force of Nature and its effect on the human sphere of activity", which is the hidden and essential meaning of Tai Chi.

As we study Nature's activities we experience the euphony of her strides as she performs her work with an impressive unification of energies as outlined in the evolutionary wizardry that has given life to a milliard of life-forms found in the air, land, and sea. We watch wonderstruck as she maintains stable and predictable patterns as evidenced in the creative displays of her balanced and faultless exhibitions of planetary movements and galactic inter-relatedness.

Certainly, man bears witness to the transforming effects as seen through the complex fabric of organic and environmental interactions, of which he is an indivisible part. Yet from the story of man's conduct and undertakings, human beings act as though they live in an isolated zone which is non referential. It is important to recognize that man is a dynamic organism with a direct communicating channel to the intricate workings of natural order.

Essentially, the individual is a subsystem interacting within the transformative matrix of nature's milieu. Man's tie to nature may be considered the most pertinent element of existence and his actions have a direct bearing on the organic and environmental structure of the Earth with consequent extensions affecting the vector of the entire universe.

This dynamic inter-relationship is the quintessential feature of oriental philosophy and belongs to an ancient method of understanding the nature of cosmic inter-relatedness and underscores man's need to avoid unbridled extremism.

This system of knowledge, which is at once a contemplative approach to self-comprehension and at the same time a philosophical treatise which views man's relationship to the universe as an inherent marriage, is known as the 'Tao,' pronounced "dow."

From the cocoon of the Tao, the elements of this grand universe emerge in polychromatic diversity and from its hidden operations there is to be found an underlying field of energy which animates the vital force that supports the human body's organic functions. Evolution is predicated by the reserves and strength of available physiological energy. Furtherstill, each living being is endowed with "consciousness" and is enlivened by the degree of psychic clarity which the individual can enlarge upon through the course of his/her life.

The individual represents the seed of civilization and as lucid and empowered as the individual is, so run the affairs of society as a whole.

Let us consider the efficacy of Tai Chi practice as a method of approach which will fortify the mind and strengthen the body, so as to better deal with the onslaught of modern activity and bring us one step closer to providing positivity to a darkening world order. The direction cannot be so much in the manipulation and orchestration of inert matter, but needs to expand to a return toward natural order and to the fertile fields of self-awareness.

Nature is a *living* system, a polymorphous entity whose infinite wavelengths and vibrations paint the canvas of the universe. Her invisible seeds proceed to impregnate the world with ever-changing forms of higher degrees of order.

One of these *seeds*, in a manner of speaking, has grown to become her guardian. For it is that the human being is an intrinsic element which contributes to the balance of forces in the scheme of organic and universal operations.

Although the pace of human evolution seems strained and slow, we are nevertheless being swept along by cosmic currents and astrochemical forces that unite us and propel our journey "home."

The substance of this inter-relationship can be found in the ancient Chinese canons of the 'Hui Ming Ching.' The inference points to an inherent alliance between man and the operations of cosmic and natural order and moreover defines a pathway to the substrata of the unconscious wherein lies the primal source of being. This innate unification points to an evolutionary pattern which allows the individual to climb the ladder of elevated consciousness where personal actions can become more spontaneous, intuitive, and free from mechanical behavior.

The Tao, which can been viewed as the 'way' to natural order, denotes a search for self-harmony, while its central purpose is the attainment of liberated self-awareness and the intensification of conscious life.

"...to impregnate the world with ever-changing forms of higher degrees of order."

As a philosophy, the Tao holds the most important secrets of Chinese thinking. The lessons of the Tao are based on the practical insights evolved from the ancient cultural life of China and issue forth from the highly gifted minds of the Chinese, whose conceptual framework is suffused with profound insights and intuitive ingressions revealing the nature of the human mind and the state of the human soul.

This exploration in self-reality requires that the student apply himself resolutely to the task of natural self-order, which is dynamically represented in the mind-body fusing of the Tai Chi approach.

The quagmire of methods aspiring toward 'self-hood' are replete with oftentimes delusive directives which promise "nirvanic" transformations. It is only with diligent application and sound integrity that the aspirant can hope to avoid the bog of philosophical flirtations expounded by the exaggerated sentiments of superstitious mystics.

There is an ancient Chinese saying which succinctly offers this advice; "If the wrong man uses the right means, the right means works in the wrong way!"

When considering the wisdom of Chinese thinking, it may very well be advised that the reader need not assume that those of us in the West require imitating Chinese culture per se, but rather to allow those qualities and predilections in our psyche, which may be used for self-potentiation, to merge with less familiar methods employed for self-awareness.

Through this amalgamation, we can enlarge our capacity to understand the nature of the human mind and in turn begin a dialogue with our innate connection to a more profound universal directive.

The concordance of transformational rules, used for the climb to self-awareness, as exists in Eastern and Western schools of thought, can lead the individual who is sincerely committed, to a more complete level of self-development related to emotional, physical and psychological self-order.

Through the aesthetic discipline of the Tai Chi methodology, there comes a growing sense of individualism, and the 'journey in mindfulness' begins to resonate with the underlying current of nature.

As Carl Jung pointed out: "Self-growth is dependent on the assimilation of the unknown!"

Through the acculturation of the Tai Chi discipline, there comes a growing recognition that the human being is not a separate part of the universe, not an isolated grain of sand washed upon the shores of a temporal and dispensable world and somehow tucked away, as it were, in some remote corner of the cosmos, but is in actuality a being that thrives for self-affirmation while possessing a spirit that seeks triumph through cooperation. As a living organism, human beings are sentient creatures that are in reality integral components who figure crucially in the great mechanism of universal operations.

Tai Chi represents a system of learning that will help us cross the great gulf between acquired knowledge and inherent wisdom, between reason and intuition, whilst qualitatively breathing new life into the meaning of cultural exchange.

Here we see a multi-disciplinary system which dynamically approaches the transformative process of self-awareness and proceeds from the physical range of bodily coordination to the refined psychological plateaus of elevated awareness.

The process of life is not merely one of birth, dreaming and dying. Man's deep urge to understand the riddle of creation and his place and purpose in this pristine universe has been a powerful and driving force taking him to the summit of ingenuity and to the touchstone of humility. There are times when he commands with vision and there are times when he gropes in the dark, and perhaps, in his endless search for self-realization, he will see the pieces of his life fall into the great jigsaw of creation.

For Man, the way home remains obscured by the clouded violence that confronts each of us on the journey through life. There are those who have come to live with the brutality of existence and still others who have somehow endured the severity of circumstances that are daily played out in the human arena of monstrous plans and in the pandemonium of outworn speculations, and finally in the self-inflating atmosphere of vainglorious vapors.

In this late hour of self-appointed superiority, amidst our pregnant cocoons of calibrated computers, we feel the spell of sterility and the death of nature's broad and wondrous lessons. The journey home is crowded with inordinate hungers that evoke a cyclopean greed that swallows human compassion.

The wave of events have drawn man out beyond his depth and he is left struggling to find a foothold in a drifting whirlpool of specious and wanting communication.

We watch helplessly as the great social-machine rolls mercilessly along, spoils to the conquerors, as they palter over the distribution of wealth; an insidious and terrible game to play with the homeless and the hungry who have been removed from their natural right to share our banquet.

It has been asserted that we are destined to know the dark beyond the stars before we comprehend the nature of our own journey.

From the forgotten to the unexpected - from the vault of memories to the treasure-chest of fantasies - from life to death, we are caught in the wondrous web of the unknown and find ourselves surrounded by the clinging threads of uncertainty that make up the substance of our existence.

"We are caught in the clinging threads of uncertainty that make up the substance of our existence."

Infinite Reflection

"Softness triumphs over hardness,
gentleness over dominance.
What is more pliable wins over
that which is rigid.
This is the principle of handling
things by going along with them;
of mastery through adaptation."

— Lao Tsu

It has been conjectured that the Sea has given birth to the inheritors of the Earth.

There are those who come to drink of her waters so as to replenish their strength and continue their short and often desperate stay upon this ocean-planet. They can never begin to realize that within the very liquid that quenches their terrible thirst may very well be the father and mother of their nativity.

Then again, above, lie the expansive galaxies with their speeding sentinels charging through the soundless dark that envelopes the Earth. Millions of terrestrial years beyond us we find the nether worlds of countless stars on the verge of birth and death and of racing planets that respect the boundaries of collision.

Man has long risen from hands and knees, thereby enabling his fingers to explore, manipulate and modify his environment to specifications that suit his need for protection and power. Now he reaches his inventive hand into the future and has created a plethora of exotic machines that serve his every need as demanded by his activities in the external world.

"Above us and below us are countless stars on the verge of birth and death."

But let us not forget that the magnificent mechanisms of the human body are products of an ancient hidden teaching taken from an organic alphabet that was born in eternity. The biological trail of instructions have been received on a molecular level, deep below the threshold of our ordinary waking consciousness. Yet, we have come to see that man is not so much unique as a creature, but rather as part of a continuum; a legacy which places him at the helm of the animal kingdom.

Man is a variant of the code of life, beginning perhaps, as some may figure, a brainless sponge that gave birth to a novel type of species; a species whose eyes reflect the presence of a mind - a soul!

We have been altered by time and circumstance and from the esoteric bank of universal instructions, Nature imposes her mighty will on the evolutionary process. She extends herself through unrivaled creative impulses that strike deep into the genetic code of every living thing, and She alone is responsible for the life-giving force that causes every animated being to pace the dimensions of the material world.

Somewhere within the atomic darkness there is a cryptic language that transmits its messages from one generation to the next, delicately, dramatically, altering the corporeality of each species: lengthening the neck - stretching the tongue - shortening the finger. Each living entity continues to change in subtle degrees, but never to return to its original form.

Man stares into the black dome of space partaking of the ultimate wonder of life and has come to realize that he represents only a small piece of the puzzle in the realm of existence. Man is, after all, only a visitor, a guest whose time is reflected in the dismal caves of his Neanderthal beginnings.

Still, he searches, not only toward the heavens for some clue as to the meaning of life, but wonders at the peculiarity of the bright red liquid oozing from an unfortunate cut in his foot.

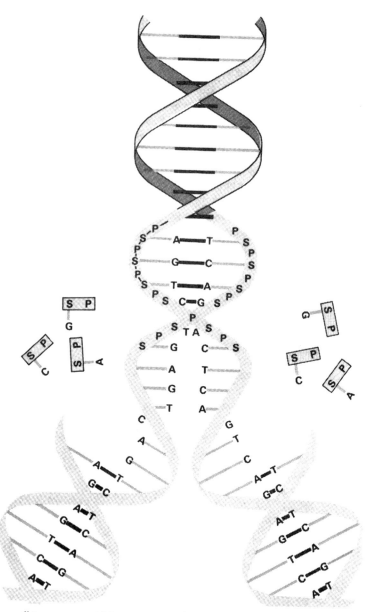

"Are we nothing more than a chance sequence in the roulette of genetic factors?"

Man has penetrated and discovered vast new realities and has reached into the swarming cells of his own body, which also gather to make sense of the situation and act to protect him from an environment which is hostile and hungry and invisible. Man has landed from the sea, or perhaps from some far-off place in cosmic space. Still, wherever his starting point, he is here as one who seeks a message, some sign, that will help him find the way home, using the gifts he was given long before his memory of self.

Man is an illusion of form that momentarily surfaces upon the old face of the Earth and then slips beneath its rocky surface, forgotten as it were, save for the silent message left written in the genetic library that the future will play upon.

Are we a little world lost in a small corner of the universe and our time, but a blink in the eye of the cosmos? Are we little more than a random event, a chance sequence in the roulette of genetic factors? Can we believe that the sea is the amphitheater of our birth? Do we so passionately climb trees as children because we are daring enough to imitate our ancestry?

Perhaps we will never know the beginning, but does that preclude our ability for self-comprehension and for understanding the part we play in the natural order of universal events?

Man is essentially a problem-solving entity who although organically locked into the course of evolution has nevertheless managed to engineer his future through copious servomechanisms of his own invention. However, he has come to see that in order to scale the higher rungs of evolution he must transcend the narrow workings of an under-developed ego and gain access to the deeper inroads of the unconscious stations of the mind.

As we mature and improve our standing in life, there rises an awareness that the ego represents a lopsided component on the field of awareness.

The ego is an occupational component of the mind, working within the confines of a conditioned pattern imposed by contemporaneous social injunctions and concurrent models for behavior. The ego simply imitates life and describes a reduced aspect of reality.

There is a personal responsibility in cultivating a clear and central consciousness which also recognizes that life is certainly greater than the territory belonging to the ego-bound mind.

The individual is lost, as it were, in the superfluidity of countless directions dictated by the investigable realities of the ego's mechanical dictates.

Our concern must surely lie beyond a construct of reality which can be contemplated and yet we appear not to be able to truly live in the truth of that meditation. The struggle to attain what we already are may seem ridiculous, since we believe ourselves to possess an awareness of *all* that we actually are.

The Tao presents us with an understanding of human life that is connected to the creative will to become **authentic**. The real interest here lies in breaking free of those inextinguishable impulses which prevent us from reaching the essence of our being.

And yet in the face of social machinations, it all comes down to an endless movement that proceeds from what seems to be obvious, to that which is disquietingly equivocal. There is no calm realm of truth, nor is there a sense of a permanent self, and the contents of consciousness are spilled into perpetual confusion and ultimately dissatisfaction.

The wheel of private awareness proceeds with 'mind-nails' driven into self-obscurity, and for many there is an unsettled desire to move out of an immobility of what is simply a 'dialectic of spirit.'

"Life takes on a stifled aspect when lived in relation to social platitudes and generalized conformity."

Life takes on a stifled aspect when lived in relation to social platitudes and generalized conformity. Somewhere it begs us to move beyond the weighty and pretentious mechanisms of intellectualism which abandon us to a tension between what is ideological, and the total range of all that is genuinely possible.

That which confronts us is a 'realm-of-reason' that is restricted to a banquet of bromides and the endless technicality in what is expected of us. We respond to what is correct and to the plan laid down by those who would ask us to remain secure in the numbing awareness of our pressing limits.

The **now** of things finds us bound to a consciousness in favor of endless claims and validities taken from the bowels of scientific conjecture.

We are close to seeing that this 'technological orbit' has at length created a corrupt distance in human intimacy. We seem compelled to ingest the scraps of specialized information of a permutating system of knowledge which leaves us to crawl through the narrowing sphere of empirical existence. We are left to traverse the growing borders of the 'digital-realm' and are presented with an emporium of potentialities, while teased with ceaseless possibilities that crowd for attention.

Here is the promise for happiness and here are the instruments of the future which finally remain indifferent to us and categorically serve their own mutant strength.

Since these issues are in any case tangential to our primary topic, and in the main far too technical for presentation in this essay, let us study the relationship of human hope and disposition in the realm of existence.

What is authentically possible is sharpening our awareness of our limits and discovering the source, or essence of what can be posed as, "My being and the power through which I am genuinely myself."

This elusive state of being, oftentimes called the 'self,' which has come to be identified as the 'individual,' is always present, even though it largely remains discreet. If the singular self does in fact exist, and is not so much just another wandering through the philosophical plasma of an ideological perspective, then we have only the arm of heightened awareness by which to reach it, so as to make our way back to the beginning of who we are.

It is a return to the wellspring of a primal secret which brings to us the healing truth of self-identity. This is the fount of 'self-reality' which reaches beyond the dynamics of social and cultural conditioning and may be seen as the **substance** of self-expression. The self appears to be an incalculable identity and is more graspable when expressed through the actions of the personality, and it is this definition that is representational of the individual.

Still, 'individuality' is a misleading term, since the individual does not remain true to **one** identity and is more or less an assembly of entities, or personalities, that forage through the world via a multiplicity of moods and feelings. The individual is, after all, a staccato of disparate emotional and mental energies emerging, in rare moments, as one conscious and whole being, and sporadically animated by one intelligence.

Let us strive to realize that the **entirety** of man is a collection of psychic and metabolic agencies, as it were, and each of the physical structures, along with the metaphysical tentacles and invisible wires of mind, may well be seen as sectional and distinct organic components, or even as a conglomeration of 'living entities.'

"Man is an assembly of entities, moving with metaphysical tentacles - seeing with the invisible wires of his mind."

This is certainly not limited to physical structures and also includes the sentimental encasements which compose our emotional content. Through the wondrous intelligence peculiar to 'thinking man,' there is a sense of wholeness that is created through our attempt to string together the emotional and psychological experiences of our life-pattern.

Regretfully, at this stage in human development, a discrete and lone status which identifies a **whole** individual is a rare occurrence and largely conjectural.

Nonetheless, the aim of Tai Chi is an evolution toward a state of self-homogenity and points to a self-containment which draws together the myriad aspects that formulate the curious creature called man.

Through the ingressive lessons of Tai Chi, we become more inclined to develop a level of self-focus that acts to balance the inwardness of self with the outwardness of the persona. The interplay between the private self and the public individual finds an equable interconnectedness as our actions manifest with greater fluency in the external world of deeds and accomplishments.

Through Tai Chi practice we incite the conception of new cycles of personal growth and are more opened to moving toward a greater range of experiences. Our growing awareness of a more complete self is a prelude to drawing the lines of our own evolution.

What man is and what he can become is a fundamental question that is more dependent on discerning the difference between 'essence' and 'personality,' and once this distinction is grasped a pathway will be set for establishing a certainty that the individual lacks in knowing himself.

As it stands, the individual remains hidden in defensive mechanisms and inversions that separate him from his fellow man. He endures the bareness of stifled emotions in the rarely completed activity of cursory communication which buries any possibility of an intimate approach. He finds himself relegated to the realm of hidden and defensive tactics that further ensnare him in negative emotions, and escape is sought in the weighted rhythm and confusion of activity.

The real scope is to work upon the rails of self-ingression and feel the cadence of the 'inner-train' of awareness; to ride beyond disquietude and listen to the sound of the inward-wheels of natural and spontaneous movement in their rhythmic clicking across the trestles of self-certainty, echoing against the hillside of self-reality.

Clearer becomes the way, as we move into the distant mountains of elevated consciousness that are lush with the scent of a virgin earth; awareness sated with the rising mist of self-knowledge and life wet with edifying rain.

Once we hop upon the ancient rails of self-comprehension, there comes the opportunity to expand the boundaries of consciousness, and thus migrate toward the horizon of self-illumination. Through this transit in awareness, we may hope to reach a state of emotional equilibrium and perhaps cipher the mystery of our real purpose in the scheme of living. We may look into the old face of the universe and see the message written in the stars that live and grow just as we do; "Be what you are and shine as nothing else!"

There is another more private pathway where some are bold enough to tread amongst the stars within, and discover the hidden universes that await; those who would dare break the shackles of ordinary consciousness.

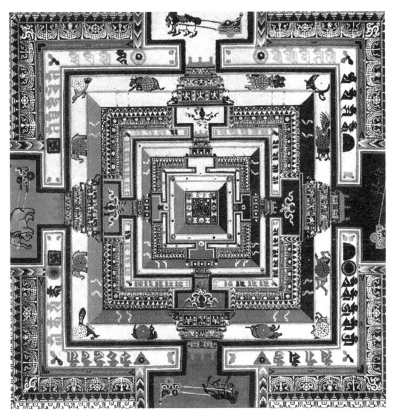

"In this irenic sanctuary we are romancing awareness through the mystery of self-being."

There are those who will retreat and seek refuge in a hidden dialogue, where they are found embracing revolutionary vibrations, that evolve to become the touchstones of energy that succor and promote innovative personal growth.

In this irenic sanctuary we are romancing awareness through the mystery of self-being.

The problems that stand in the way of meaningful self-reality are ultimately tied into the tools that man is to use for discovering the seed of self-purpose.

Man's measured strides are saddled with convolutions and dilemmas that affect his potential on the social, psychic and organic levels.

Finding one's essential goal and the potential strength to reach beyond the limits of requisitioned security and regulated structure are the keys that will channel forth the answers necessary for a quantum change.

Eventually, as a race of beings, we must take on a far more subtle enigma; for the problem that faces man is the conundrum of **destiny**. Are we heading in a direction that will correct the balance between the inner world of individual self-hood and the grosser workings of the personality that play in the realm of unyielding patterns?

Are we prepared to turn our heads toward the faint ticking of the universal wheel that will help us cross the terrain of timorous formalism? Can we discover that each living thing is an essence and exists to demonstrate a new present?

In the resolute application of focused awareness, we can begin to draw from the inner reservoirs of psychic inspiration, as well as extract power from the well of physical vitality. This will enable us to produce a vehicle for creative self-change, and without the fear of losing harmonious proportion.

This is the empyrean of Promethean spirits that sail into the sun of self-reality. We must discover the appropriate tool for self-discovery, and as we acquaint ourselves with vaster spaces and cosmic criteria, we can begin to experience a progressive petalling of awareness.

The way to the self is to find greater modesty in our conquests, or be crushed by the forces we have created, which can neither be held steady, nor assimilated to our being. To carry on to the true self is to become part of the cosmic polyphony that carries beyond the gulches that the ego has conjured.

Man's purpose is to step beyond the failing orbit of 'disabled awareness' so that the mind can become suffused with novel approaches and creative mental formulations that will trigger a concomitant expansion of consciousness.

We have only the power of our mind and the force of spirit, in the final analysis, to go forward and must take the necessary measures that will fortify our journey in self-hood; for only in the immeasurable space of ideas does man become real to himself.

As put so well by Frank Barron, "The sorcery and charm of imagination and the power it gives to the individual to transform his world into a new world of order and delight, makes it one of the most treasured of all human capacities."

Therefore let the individual guard his mind well so as to find the seed of transcendent intelligence. The experience that awaits the mindful student is one of self-transfiguration which will bring to light new ranges of encounters undreamed of before.

Tai Chi can be seen as a self-guiding technology, and through dedicated application to its principles of instruction, this system of knowledge will act to tear open the seed of deeper personal growth. In Tai Chi practice, what qualitatively develops is a new degree of mental acuity which enlivens and intensifies our conscious life. The events arising out of focused-awareness will lead the student to an enhanced level of self-growth which comes about as a direct result of a creative modification from within.

"Tai Chi guides the student inward to a peaceful oasis of self-order through a creative modification within."

Studious application clears a trail for transformation and self-renewal and serves to guide the student inward to a peaceful oasis of self-order.

Focused-awareness carries the aspirant to a hidden glen beyond the chillbreath of insatiable wanderings that monopolize the mind. There comes into existence a re-patterning of the mind and a reevaluation of the very aim and meaning of mental activities.

It is not merely a quantitative difference that replaces the old model of thinking. It has more to do with an opportunity to penetrate the wall of the ego-bound mind.

Through this ingression the student will begin to cultivate a self-authenticity, an individualism if you will, that is more passionately capable of seeing beyond the cubicled existence found in the redundancy of a compulsive world which is graphically one of imitation and uniformity; a world in which we find the individual merely 'covering ground' through bare intellectual movement.

This is a difficult picture to view. And the seemingly harsh light shed upon the old and tired pattern of behavior is very much a portrait of the individual who is frozen in emotional guarding; seen shaking in obedience to rules and regulations which are indifferent to him. Regrettably, the individual in his expression of his deepest inwardness almost seems to have vanished.

We have only managed to create a world which is principally dedicated to mental tasks and intellectual endeavors, while the depth of our emotions linger in the narrow corridors of overcrowded bookstalls. The fate of our passions are too often left in the hands of booksellers and storytellers, while we vicariously survive on the melodramatic morsels thrown to us from the elevated platforms of theater.

We resign ourselves to the darkened arena and safety of the cinema and are saddled to the devices of our imagination.

We are given, as it were, a facsimile of emotional content. What little there is of reality, is lost in a drifting crowd of faceless people shuffling through the tasteless popcorn and half-torn ticket-stubs that stand as discarded reminders of reality. We stare blankly, reminded of the life we somehow cannot seem to live.

But still, there is a struggle that is raging in the deepest strata of the heart and an attempt to move to **higher ground** is vitally necessary, in spite of the fear that it will lay bare the inadequacy of our whole effort.

Who are we when our energy is spent taking aim at living someone else's life?

We are trapped in an attempt to reach a new position in our quest for self-reality! We are left in a reconciliation between the actual and pretended, and our struggle is to make the situation not only tolerable, but somehow more clearly intelligible.

As we wade through the waters of self-doubt we are lambently touched by ripples of awareness that remind us that we have placed great emphasis on defining ourselves as rational creatures. We are, after all, intellective beings whose power is inarguably present in our capacity to shape the world through extravagant tools and artificial devices. We are anthropocentric, bold little creatures who imagine that the human intellect is the yardstick against which all other living things must compare themselves.

"How do we step beyond the calculated cleverness of technology which has failed to unite us as complete human beings and has simply tied us together as intellectual entities?"

Yet, with all our intellectual power and manipulative skill we have not reached beyond hatred or revenge, or the desire to dominate.

It might be wise to remember that our mental energy is born from the shadowy powers behind nature; our strength rising from the depths of the consciousness of being. Yet 'being,' invariably surrenders to the dictates of the ego, and remains at the disposal of the ego, which is amended by the direct influence of the immediate geography and social criteria of the individual's world in question.

What becomes of us is altogether modified according to the medium of consciousness which remains locked into perceptions that are perpetually influenced by the sounds and sights of the external and material components of life.

Who we are remains an anemic residue, and what we are to become is directly influenced and revived through the trigger-perceptions of contemporaneous images and words, which are stored in the warehouse of awareness.

What we are can be summed up in the experiences of our **perceptions;** which reach into the past of our emotional content.

Our lives are fed by complacent acceptance of the 'norm' and reinforced by the things we read and listen to, and then again, by whether these perceptions have been pleasurable or harsh. We are therefore left to words and deeds that have left us to soften the grating reality of our feelings of isolation. Our need is to announce and uncover the awkwardness we live with as we make our way through the dim reality of mechanical awareness.

In our attempt to communicate what we are as sentient beings, we have at our behest the monumental endowment of speech. It is language and its intelligent applications that identifies our history, and in a truer sense, what little we understand of our reality.

There are few creatures other than man who are capable of both syllabification and the use of modulated sounds to express distinctive and exact shades of thought, if not feeling. In effect, our ability to speak has shaped the mind of man. Further still, this legacy in communicative dexterity, however limited by personal scope and fluency, has led us to the prodigiously contemplative skill which allows us to 'color our reflections.' That is to say, our thoughts are perpetuated infinitely by our ability to 'write,' which is the taken-for-granted-medium that allows, for example, this writer to reach across the invisible medium of space and time and communicate directly with you.

These endowments, belonging to words, being the left and right sides of the great seesaw of hearing and speaking with the mind, grant us the opportunity to sign our feelings and our ideas implicitly, and in turn to pass our messages, fraught with meaning, and deliver ageless symbols that are saturated with legacy, to successive and cherished generations.

Still, there is an inherent quality in man that surpasses these noteworthy talents that rest under the umbrella of our intellect.

Can we agree that the intellect is after all principally a frontier component of the mind that tries to mediate between the outer world and the realm of the unconscious? The intellect can often be seen to stride with gallant maneuvers in an attempt to make the world fall in line with emotional content.

For the most part the individual sees himself deserted by all protective forces; hence the assertions of the intellect come to the rescue. The intellect clothes unconscious demands with its conscious rationalizations, tempering the admonitions of reality, while disguising the individual's conflicts with the world around him, and finally makes its 'primate' calculations based on menacing perceptions and bends to compliant, opportunistic, and deceitful methods of behavior.

This is not to ignore the higher, moral, suprapersonal side of human nature and therefore this line of approach will now proceed to investigate the whereabouts of the higher side of human nature.

Somewhere in that contemplative moment, concealed behind the weighted curtain of the unconscious, before hand touches pencil, in advance of lead striking paper, a human being sees that no matter how broad his intellect, his authentic power can be found in *self-reflection*. Here is the mirror of self-comprehension, and it is in that silent state of psychic limbo, in that pristine moment, that we see how the mind reaches outward toward a higher mode of being.

We reach for an idealized state where we are no longer tempted to draw back from ourselves and are suffused with an overwhelming desire to make clear the difference between what is real and what is pretended, between the outer and the inner.

For one brief moment we become elevated in eternity and at the same time we fall gracefully inward, surrendering to the mindfulness of self-comprehension. We are left in the realm of self-reflection which unites the heart and mind and we find ourselves moving along the sea of the infinite, having finally given up land.

This is the journey of the human-ship moving toward the horizon of wholeness, sailing enigmatically across the ancient mind-currents of time and space; the captain anticipating, listening, with the *inner-eye*, watching from the dark chasm of his universal mind, looking for the shores of self-reality. He stands at the helm waiting for the hidden message that will answer the question to finding out what he is not yet and how to prepare for being it.

The underlying truth that points the way 'home' was summed up by Daniel Webster when he said, "Mind is the great lever of all things; human thought is the process by which human ends are ultimately answered."

Where is the knowledge to self-comprehension that reaches beyond the spiritless complications of the customary trials of the modern city?

Where is the awareness that does not fall into the quiet of the expected and the established, nor stops at the endless ambiguity of trivial pursuit?

Whatever the answer to these questions, it will lie beyond the cold and blurred dynamics of modernity with its noise and dust. The resolution will carry above the muted pleas of cerebral spirituality and past the febrile rantings of moralizing religion.

For it is, that final elucidations can only be heard in the private chamber of the individual mind and uniquely found within the grotto of the solitary heart.

We can hope that one day we will break out of the 'prison of the finite,' and the sound of truth will at last break the lonely journey of self-doubt. We are by now familiar with the journey, inured to the peculiar hardships of contending with everyday life, but let us reach beyond the illusion where the preciseness of technology and the correctness of science is confused with the meaning of truth.

Let us view the present state of cultural affairs, which brings into view that we are living as prisoners in a paradoxical reality; we have become victims of our fascination with discovery, cleverness, and novelty.

Yes, we have reached the ultimate paradox: seemingly able to understand nearly the whole of nature and yet we remain incapable of understanding the nature of being human - and here we are, caught in these strange and curious times where the average citizen is left struggling to understand the mounting dialogue of technology and is left bewildered by the labyrinthine conclusions of a runaway science.

The lessons of Tai Chi are cumulative in their impact as they give way to greater self-composure and can act as a qualifying stabilizer in modern man's convoluted path along the time-stream of the future.

Let us endeavor to grasp the veracity of 'self-reality' and discover that the way to truth can become a more exciting task. Let us wander through the milky dust of countless galaxies, across the brine of twinkling space, where we can hear faint callings of celestial symphonies and cryptic astral sounds that seem to issue forth from an imposing assembly of lights that offer a staggering view of a stupendous solar system. Let us peer into a vast and boundless space that is millions of light years in the future.

As small as we are in the scheme of things, we are part of a priceless balance that identifies us as the offspring-travelers gliding through the crystal palace of space.

We are the thistledown and milkweed fairies who ride upon the blue wind of evening twilight venturing into new domains. Like wavering shadows, we hope to reach beyond the psychical limitations of our insubstantial reality, and somehow we know that in each of us there lies the secret of the universe.

Is there an answer behind the grand canopy of stars that will raise our trials to a smile?

Counter-Movements
of the
Wondrous Automaton

*"One must learn to crawl
before one can stand -
Stand before one can walk -
Walk before one can run -
and one must think-
before attempting anything!"*

— ancient Chinese adage

On the first day of meeting my teacher, even before committing myself to any practice, I sat before him in an open garden and I respectfully asked, "Shifu Shan, how long will it take me to become accomplished in the movements of Tai Chi?"

Shifu Shan quietly answered, "About ten years!"

I cautiously continued, "Now what if I practice diligently morning and evening, every day. . . how long then?"

Without looking at me he calmly responded, "Twenty years!"

I was flustered by Shifu Shan's answer, so I raised my voice emphatically, retorting, "What if I practice faithfully, working twice as hard as all your other students, both day and night, summer and winter, and with all my strength, how long then?"

At this point Shifu Shan's eyes widened and he finally turned his gaze to me and with an unchanging expression on his face peacefully said, "Thirty years!"

I sat dumbstruck for a moment and then turned my head away and looked up into the sky, as though an answer lay hidden in the lining of a drifting cloud. "But . . . Shifu Shan . . . !" I turned to him holding back my impatience; hoping to make sense of his private logic and pursued my course, "I fail to understand!"

I took a deep breath and continued haltingly, "How can it be . . . that customarily it takes ten years to become adept . . . and then if I practice diligently, it will take me twenty years to master the events and maneuvers . . . and if I work harder than all the other students, day and night, it will take me thirty years!" I swallowed my irritation and continued, " Please honorable teacher, open my eyes to this way of thinking!"

Shifu Shan slowly rose to his feet, then carefully took me by my shoulders and raised me to his level, **then slowly brought his face only inches from mine and abruptly said,** "With one eye on the goal, you have only one eye with which to learn!"

At this point Shifu Shan and I just stood there looking at each other. Then slowly, our bodies began to shake like a rising tide that was about to engulf us, as we erupted into a tumultuous fit of volcanic laughter. At the same moment the sun broke through a thin veil in the hazy brightness of the morning air.

The tradition of Tai Chi has had a long and prominent history of evolution and development. From the time of the founder of Chinese surgery, physician Hua T'o, (190 A.D.) up until the present day, the Tai Chi method of approach, in its varied physical outcroppings, has appeared in various forms, as seen in a plethora of martial-art styles, past and present.

Students of the writings of Tai Chi Chuan are being challenged by a swelling bed of evidence that has created convolutions in the ethical attempts to place this 'internal' martial art into a proper historical perspective.

Flowing over one side of its chronicled banks are a slew of fanciful derivatives that have worked their way through the layers of interest belonging all at once to the directives of what is fashionable, marketable, and ideological, while on its opposing bank, the waters are swollen with the prejudices of lineage and legend.

If we are left to look through the dim fog of partiality as to Tai Chi's inauguration and transplantation, let us then mark the work of scholars who generally agree that the "apple-wagon" must have been delivered to, or advanced by, the Chen family of the celebrated Chen village in Honan province, and later appropriated by Yang Lu-Shan, (d. 1799-1872) who worked for the Chen family in the capacity of something like a house-boy or floor-mopper and peered over the high walls of secrecy and spied on the choreography of the 'offspring-clan-only' teachings of a powerful style of movements belonging to this intricate martial style. The Chen family discovered Yang practicing with great skill and marvelled at Yang's facility with such complex maneuvers and in consideration that he was never given any lessons. Indeed Yang Lu Shan would later receive official instruction due to his remarkable talent.

According to legend, Tai Chi Ch'uan is credited to Chang San-Feng (d. 1314), who acquired his skills at a Shaolin monastery. However, as history would remark it was one Chiang Fa who passed on the Tai Chi system, then called Tao-Yin (dow-yeen), to the eminent Chen family of whom Chen Wang-Ting (d. 1618) is considered the originator.

Tai Chi has certainly grown through the efforts of the illustrious Yang family and it was Yang Lu-Shan who received instruction from Chen Chang-Shin. In its well-guarded evolution it has managed to split into three main branches, that being the Chen, Yang and Wu styles, named so simply because of the family name of its founders. Tai Chi has made an escape into a small number of diverse forms, as seen in the Wuu, Sun and Li styles, all of which have nevertheless grown out of respect to the forerunners and sages of antiquity.

Beginning with Master Chang San-Feng to general Chen Wang-Ting, who are among the notable founders, the tradition has been elaborated by other lesser known teachers such as Wang Tsun, Chen Tun-Chow, Yeh Chi-Ma and Wang Tsun-Yueh, who were nevertheless outstanding artists and teachers who produced splendid formulations with varying emphasis on Tai Chi's key tenets.

Those sturdy individuals who made up the ranks of the Tai Chi armada were broad-minded men who devoted themselves untiringly to the martial arts, and their motives were as mixed as the families that bore their names.

Some protected convoys of wealthy landowners, some acted as paladins for the ruling class, while others were simply bodyguards for the moneyed merchants whose nails were too long to hold a weapon.

The familiar tenor of family feuds, national revolution, and the insipid elements of racial purging were not beyond the scope of these trying times that witnessed still others who found themselves smack in the middle of the machinations, and used the principles of Tai Chi pugilism to deal with the sordid insurgencies.

Entry into the twentieth century found the Chinese embroiled in a revival of martial fitness to cast off Manchu domination and counter Japanese and Western Imperialism.

With the cultural revolution sparking out in 1973 and seemingly ended by the late 1980's, there is greater freedom of expression in Mainland China; where patrons of the Shao-Lin Taoist priest Chang San-Feng are claiming genesis of the Tai Chi system, with jingoism gathering in the martial centers of Shanghai and Beijing.

At the other end of the China Sea, Taiwan had absorbed the exodus of the sages and teachers of the Taoist and Buddhist based systems of fighting who fled China during the latter part of the cultural revolution. It is here that the Taiwanese continue to lift the flag of historical perspective announcing 300 years of glorious battles on the terra firma of Tai Chi and asserting Tai Chi's advent to be the work of the Chen family.

While, today, Tai Chi Chuan is predominantly seen as a kind of meditation in movement, it has mostly resisted being reduced to classification. Still, it may be characterized as a conduit of Chinese metaphysics and medicine rolled into the core of a martial science.

Yes, speculation as to the inception of this 'work of art' remains abstracted, however its philosophical underpinnings are clearly based on two circles of latitude: one is anecdotal and replete with familial elitism and hero-worship; while the other is medical and abounds with theories and exercises that proffer healthful longevity, and extends into claims for immortality that border on the mystical.

The mythical presentation revolves around the offering of the work by an enlightened teacher or immortal, whereas the medical approach articulates the vigorous operations of Chinese culture in the anthropocentric battle with disease and infirmity.

The martial arts have been broadcast and propagated by two schools: one being the Wu-Tang (woo dang) method and the other being the Shao-Lin (shaow lin) system.

At the same time there is only one tree that represents Tai Chi, and we must always remember that its three main branches, those being the Chen, Yang and Wu schools, have grown from its great singular trunk.

Perhaps the most intimate parts of these ancient systems have not been transmitted purely intact, but there is something else to be considered—the gathering vultures from the present generation.

What Tai Chi was, one, two, and three hundred years ago, with its meaty succulence of energy and power rolled into the dynamic choreography of martial application, is now a diffused bundle of spiritless movements belonging to students seeking the 'external,' and individuals who have bastardized the original structures, principles, and intent of a carefully constructed system of movements and ideas.

Now "Masters-of-Tai-Chi" are popping out of the woodwork with their fatuous additions and near-sighted alterations and are bestowing upon a gullible public that 'personal touch,' which is that of a Medusa; freezing the character of Tai Chi's original mental spirit, as well as its authentic physical compositions with innovations, mistakes, and omissions.

These they dare pass on as true transmissions.

As in any language there is the pitfall of passing on errors, but the real danger is in the augmentation or erasing of information based on self-proclaimed mastery and self-professed wisdom.

If you are simply looking for physical exercise then perhaps we can excuse these impostors, but if you seek the interior realm of higher reason and contemplation, then you need to prepare yourself through diligent efforts with an exceptional teacher who clearly speaks and lives the language of Tai Chi.

All in all, Tai Chi has become a generic term, just as the name 'science' is representational of a large body of laws or principles that attempts to help us understand the various mechanisms of life. In this sense, Tai Chi can be seen as an isomorphic style that is based on an eclectic set of transformational rules that are more concerned with the qualitative use of internal energy rather than the quantitative exploitation of outer force.

Its philosophical leaning has played a significant role in the realms of social, cultural, ethical and health practices and beliefs found in Asian civilization. It is connected to one of the earliest sources of holistic health exercises and martial study representing the theory and praxis of adjusting and intensifying energetic vitality.

Through a selective policy of practical and artful concepts, the Tai Chi system quietly leads the student through a series of psychological and physical maneuvers which contribute to the union of vital force and consciousness. Through consistent practice, a new plateau of awareness is reached, underscoring concentration, energizing organic strength, and increasing muscular flexibility, while balancing structural alignment.

Not only does it act upon physical systems, but it moves to deepen and refine the intuitive process as practice creates an 'expanded' mental space that opens the mind-door to reflective insights.

The conventional principles are founded on the conservation and efficient control of personal energy. Its tenets suggest that the unbridled stimulation of the senses leads to a numbing of the body and a weakening of mental energy. This proposal is a call to the sobering reality of how the wasteful use of precious energy leads to our own self-undoing.

Tai Chi is an exercise in energy enhancement which is achieved through a process of re-appropriating accessible personal energy.

This is one of the primary considerations in the developmental phases of the Tai Chi method and points to the creation of a mind/body nucleus, in the sense of a concentrated force-field that can be applied to various stations of interest that are naturally left to the individual's discretion.

The Tai Chi approach attends to the mutual balance of internally directed energy, in the sense of physiological homeostasis, and its relationship to the amount of energy that is expended in outwardly directed levels of activity, as found in the balancing act of day to day activities. As articulated in the ancient lessons taken from the Chinese canons of the 'Huai Nan Zi': "Safe-guarding and protecting personal energy leads to the building and availing of energy."

Although Tai Chi is quite often viewed as a "soft," or an "internal" martial art, we must also understand that this does not imply that the movement-dynamics are torpid in nature.

The eloquent mercuriality of the movements sends one into a psychic realm of beauty that is over and above the clutter and noise of ordinary experience. Experience is customarily defined in terms of externalized conflicts and struggles, while in the avant-garde realm of Tai Chi the real drama is succinctly inward - that is to say, unfolding acts of sensitivity and insight, and inventive forms of understanding. It reaches beyond the social mesh of interactions which is typically overrun by standardization and mechanization. It is a curving inward to the depths of personal consciousness, which is perhaps one of the last sanctuaries left to the individual.

Aside from the physical descriptions that define Tai Chi as a "moving-meditation," or then again as a martial art that is practiced for self-defense, many are not familiar with the more profound psychological aspects that characterize the Tai Chi method of approach.

Essentially, Tai Chi is a humanistic teaching that speaks of proper cultivation of one's ability to stand outside the wall of egotism and to view human life in the context of a network of social relations.

Indeed, Tai Chi enlivens our capacity to act without contrivance.

To those who view Tai Chi as a reverent, or mystical occupation, it should be made clear that it is not concerned with the life beyond, nor with the powers of the supernatural, yet it leaves ample room for reaching those levels within ourselves that remain unprobed and undiscovered. Tai Chi can be more accurately seen as an agent, or device, which effectively gathers the natural and restorative forces of the body and attendantly focalizes mental energy.

This combination of storing mental and physical energies can in turn be used for therapeutic purposes.

That is to say, the student learns to gain control over the self-healing energy coursing deep within the sub-recesses of the human organism. As the practice becomes more fluent, the student penetrates to subtle planes of energy responsible for physiological equilibrium and organic homeostasis.

Tai Chi is a unique conditioning event which trains the student in those methods that access the biodynamic energies which charge and empower our physical and mental atmosphere.

The philosophical directives of Tai Chi are taken fundamentally from the 'I Ching' pronounced 'yee jing,' which is popularly translated as the 'Book of Changes."

Although the text of this celebrated work uses terms like 'heaven,' it is not a religious canon per se.

Peripherally, Tai Chi and the "I Ching" are sometimes seen as "religion," but it is not a "dress-up-and-hear-a-sermon-on-the-Sabbath" type of thing.

If there are some who wish to place Tai Chi in the category of a religion then we would have to authenticate its saints; individuals who were more like wandering vagabonds and rail-hoppers, bumming the Tao - persons who were not taken in by the smugness of inveterate attitudes, nor enticed by the snugness of predetermined postulations.

Rather than being mistakenly seen as priests, they were far better recognized as warriors who invented a pugilistic dance, a metaphorical battle against the enemies of sincerity and spontaneity.

And, although as an exercise, Tai Chi begins with some premeditation and planning, it moves far beyond the sleight-of-hand in social interactions where we have reached that surrealistic peculiarity - where the persona has **replaced** the person, where the mask has **become** the face, and our present course toward human intimacy seems to lie in the twilight zone of nihilistic reality.

The 'I Ching' is however, oracular in nature and rather cryptic in dialogue, while the various commentaries have been regularly ascribed to Kung-Fu-Tze, who in the West is more commonly referred to as Confucius.

There is the usual contention as to its authorship and many scholars suggest that the originators antedate Kung-Fu-Tze by three or four centuries. Whatever the case may be, the substance of the 'I Ching' indulges in viewing the effects of cosmic forces at work in our universe and their influence on human intercourse.

The philosophical underpinnings of the 'I Ching' or the 'Book of Changes' point to a continual change that accompanies the circumstances which envelop human evolution, while suggesting that man must become more aware of his inter-relatedness to the activities of universal order. Interference with the directives of natural order, in line with the attending paradoxes, is undoubtedly a dangerous preoccupation for all the alternate futures.

While verging from the 'natural route' could prove jeopardous, what needs to be kept in mind is that Nature's course is cyclical, well-ordered, and predictable, and all things that issue forth are considered good.

The entire attitude of the 'I Ching' is tied up in the 'Doctrine of the Mean;' a pathway in thought that favors 'not going to extremes.' In essence it is a philosophy which can be summed up in viewing Humanity as a *family* and one that ideally carries on in the aim of 'perfect sincerity.'

The 'Book of Changes' is divided into texts and commentaries. The earliest writings are attributed to legendary Fu-Hsi, who created the initial dimensions of the system which was built on eight banks of information, represented by a symbolic pattern of solid and/or a bifurcated line-assembly coming under the heading of "Ba Gua."

The later texts, developed into sixty-four banks of information, are ascribed to King Wen (1171-1122 b.c.). The debate as to who conceived this complex work, or when it was inspired, has occupied scholars for many years. What is most intriguing is that no single individual, nor any collective group has signed their name on the creation of this masterly document which has been more influential in the social life of the Chinese than any other text, Confucian, or otherwise.

The 'I Ching' covers a wide variety of human influences: governmental policies; social codes of behavior; political strategies; warfare; marital issues; legal relations and family affairs; to mention some of the pertinent subjects.

The line-assembly patterns, mentioned earlier, are more properly called "hexagrams", i.e. hexa (six) grams (measures), consisting of two sets of three lines (trigrams), one set atop the other, hence forming a six line tier, that stands as a marker for the eloquent essays that consistently remind us of what amounts to an *appropriate* attitude in conduct.

The philosophical orientation can be paraphrased thusly; "To persevere and be patient, and to act at the right time, is to reach a 'superior' position in attitude. Then will the individual be better prepared to deal with the inclemencies of his present situation and become endowed with the wisdom to withstand the onslaughts imposed upon him through fate."

This may seem like an oversimplification, however it points to the importance placed on attitude and destiny.

These 'six-line' markers also correspond to geographical directions, be it north, south and so on, and concur with moral qualities found in terms like: "heaven and father," "earth and mother," and extends to natural elements like 'thunder,' 'water' and 'fire.'

Single lines and their sum total are studied with their accompanying commentaries and explanations that work within the realms of philosophical and ethical meaning.

Through this perambulation, the 'I Ching' can be appreciated as taken to mean, 'path of least-resistance,' hence an *easier* route through life.

The Chinese word for *change* is 'yee,' which also means 'easy' and is usually seen written in English as 'I.'

In this way we arrive at the name "I Ching;" 'Ching' meaning 'Book.' Since *change* is the operative word, we need consider that change engenders two forces; yin, considered passive, and yang, which is weighed as active.

These intermingled concepts are often and generally considered female and male respectively.

A more pragmatic analogy which will shed more intelligible light on these sweeping abstractions would be the idea of the familiar 'two-pronged plug,' which in and of itself is technically referred to as a 'male/female relationship' as it engages an electrical outlet.

The plug accesses the surge of electricity therein and draws upon a force which is built upon a positive and negative energy-field in counter-poised relationship. This mutual reception, existing in the wires, gathers the rather dangerous force lurking in the wall. This potentially hazardous dynamism is made servile through the balanced relationship of the male and female energies that are gathered in the wires and sent along to various apparatus that perhaps light our homes, or cool the air in our bedrooms.

The same inter-relatedness gains even clearer perspective when considering that a seemingly dead car-battery can be jump-started through electrically mounting the male and female aspects of the wiring through its positive and negative poles.

Ultimately, it is the quality of inter-relatedness and not simply the condition of polarity that finally urges the vehicle into motion.

This relationship, qualified as yin and yang, and more so its balance, gives rise to all things both subjective and objective. What is more important than seeing the oversimplification of life as the outcome of a 'dark and light', or 'male and female' interconnectedness, is that the universe is in a state of continuous and dynamic modification. It flows according to its own cycles of reference.

These cycles lead to a balance of energies, not only found in the domain of Nature, but also in human beings who are curiously moving along the ancient line of evolution.

The interaction of yin and yang need not be seen as measured religious-portions of good and evil to be meted out to mankind, as is often seen through the commands of fate, but more accurately represents a dynamic interplay of potential energy which brings about all patterns, forms, and ideas which develop in complexity; just as a single living cell grows to become a functioning entity.

In this way life is seen as a progressive development which has evolved from a simple beginning.

Instead of a universe controlled by supernatural beings that can only be encountered through sacrifice and pleading, the 'I Ching' points to a natural performance of energies that follow a methodical formula. The concept of yin and yang are fused to Taoist thinking, which above all, demonstrates humankind's honored tie to Nature's energetic forces.

Through this sublime approach in human behavior and development, we are given an opportunity to understand Mankind's conduct in relation to those laws which identify universal order. This conceptual framework refers to human orchestrations and their effect on an otherwise balanced cosmic order.

At its most fundamental level the yin/yang philosophy can lead the postulant to the fount of human creativity where one can feel his/her own nature and discover that each nature has its own ultimate. Further still, it demonstrates how the individual can reach a higher level of organization as it relates to personal action in the realm of social intercourse.

Yin and Yang is the nucleus of the Tai Chi method which is a process of development that brings into view the individual's underlying strength. This is a strength that is begotten through an alliance with the understream of living energy (chi), which is believed to sustain all organic development.

Tai Chi is often connected with the idea of 'nonresistance' which holds to the narrow and typified view held by Westerners when investigating Taoism.

In the West, Tai Chi is perceived as a "quietistic" philosophy. This dignified manner, in what might better be termed as 'the way of least resistance,' should not in any way, be confused with pacifist rhetoric of bygone days.

As one practices, what becomes patent is that this approach in human conduct penetrates dynamically into inspired activity and purposeful action. The clarity of perception and the acquired self-composure so gained helps to develop the mark of 'individuality' that will not be supplanted by the redundancy of day to day activities.

Again, Tai Chi should not be associated with some prejudicial view of the 'nothing but dreams' often found in the peripheral fields of a benign philosophical meditation, but more appropriately aims at the very depth of life and the ordering of human affairs. In this sense Tai Chi acts as an agent for developing individual strength and character. It further helps to form the fundamental basis for a more direct and sincere approach in interpersonal relatedness.

Personal vitality, focalized energy, and creative spirit, form the triplex of the Tai Chi method in self-cultivation. Sincerity and self-composure are the pillars which stand as the new level for personal expression and individual effectiveness.

With each artful step, we are taught to move beyond mechanized ordering, and within its sweeping circle of aesthetic simplicity, found in the inspired movements of the Tai Chi form-play, we are carried along toward genuine self-civilization.

Tai Chi allows us to more gently discover a deeper level of self-awareness which gracefully instills a feeling of humility and self-candor.

This is the route to finding the human heart without removing our capacity to execute our ambitions. Practice leads to an expansion of personal time and space, and we begin to understand how in some deep measure we are intimately connected to Nature's vital flow.

A new attitude develops which encourages a greater receptivity to the inherent energy which sustains the biological energies of the human organism, and this is the same outstanding energy which is responsible for the Earth's ecological balance, inclusive of those ambient factors which involve cosmological inter-relatedness.

In this sense, the energy potential extends to the biological future of the world.

The fuel for our maneuvers and activities is caught up in the idea of a boundless energy called 'chi.' Our bodies are the magical vehicles of this innate organic energy, and this vital force, recognized thousands of years ago by traditional Chinese medicine, supports our biophysical activities, healing capacities, and growth potential, which in turn are related to all our experiences, both physical and mental. This cognition puts us in touch with better understanding our responsibility to Nature herself.

In Tai Chi practice we release our energies in a sustained and quiescent stream of gestures and articulations which express our capacity to merge with the current of life.

The ancient Chinese philosophers respectfully whispered "chi" and described an inspiriting and guiding force which upheld human existence. Sages on the path of self-discovery inhaled the knowledge of the cosmos, merged with the breath of life and found it to be an incorporeal substance which nurtured the material universe.

The once hidden alphabet of the ancient language of Tai Chi reveals itself today as a dynamic form of meditation in movement. It aims at reaching the fundamental structure of the unconscious. This is accomplished through specialized fields of mental and physical control.

This method in penetrating the deeper layers of the subconscious, comes under the more antique heading of *'Chi-Kung'*, (pronounced 'chee goong'), which is a celebrated health-care approach and is a direct outgrowth of the oldest medical system in the world, namely acupuncture. Its methodology dates back to emperor Huang Ti, circa 2700 b.c.

Tai Chi is an extension of the *Chi Kung* medical approach and is articulated through a brilliant choreographic sequence which dynamically revitalizes the organic structures of the body, while the psychological benefits are derived through the principles of mental focus. There is no separation between mind and body as they dovetail to meet the creative and physical demands of the task at hand.

Despite its apparent simplicity, unearthed in the slowed techniques of martial praxis, Tai Chi transcends the typical boundaries of a martial art and indeed may be more appropriately identified as a 'martial science.'

Essentially what needs to be taken into account is the concept of *movement in relation to awareness*. This points to our outer-movements which are an expression of inner consciousness, for it is that Tai Chi is a lesson in 'kinesthesia,' expressing a process rather than a state.

Tai Chi practice is not only concerned with becoming, but also with being. At the same time, this richly crafted piece of bodily artwork offers a masterful and an exacting method of approach toward uniting the conscious aspects of the mind with the underlying structure of the subconscious. Through the practice of its ancient physical language the student establishes a pathway for the intensification of conscious life, and for seeing the cuttings of personal truth fit into the puzzle of the individual's distinct life-pattern.

This unique health care program is, as already mentioned, based on a choreographed sequence of graceful, ancient exercise techniques, and has been medically proven to maintain enduring physical health and to develop mental acuity. Tai Chi exercise strengthens the entire physiology; improving posture, energizing blood circulation, enhancing neuromuscular functioning, and accelerating the healing process of disease and infection.

This eminent Chinese martial science, reformatted and initiated by the Chinese medical system of antiquity, was elaborated upon by the founder of Chinese surgery, physician Hua T'ow, circa 190 A.D.

In summation, Tai Chi integrates martial art dynamics, techniques in mental focalization, and specialized breathing modalities taken from the traditional instructions of **Chi Kung,** and has come to be known as the 'science of moving meditation.'

Another striking feature of Tai Chi, lies in its cosmological, or spiritual implications.

In the 2nd century b.c. practitioners of Chinese internal medicine compiled a document called the **Huai Nan Zi,** which explicates that man's spiritual essence, or mental spirit if you will, remains the operative force that regulates the functional elements of his entire physiology.

Taken into the present, through these ancient holistic gleanings, Tai Chi's aim is to advance the mind to the inroads of bodily power. It stands ready to access the human storehouse of intrinsic energy, referred to in traditional Chinese medicine as *chi* (pronounced "chee").

For millennia medical practitioners have pointed to the healing provisions of *chi* and suggested that the mind is the gateway for direct communication with the workings of this innate energy-field that lies in waiting, within the chasm of the human organism. Although, at face value, Tai Chi is a physical display of creative patterns, it functions as an internal discipline which engages the discriminative faculty of mind, and progress is achieved by a method of cyclic repetition. Its practice leads to the development of a self-ordered awareness that is used to access the dynamic force of *chi* found coursing throughout the human body.

Here in the West, and speaking from a neurological standpoint, the human body is seen as an elaborate machine of interconnected wirings that is ceaselessly engaged in balancing and refining the functional elements of the brain and its electrical output to the muscular system, referred to as neuromuscular force.

In the language of Tai Chi, the body's electrical energy (*chi*) is considered to be the life-flow of the 'enchanted machine,' that is to say, the human organism.

Traditional Chinese medicine emphasizes that without the proper distribution of *chi*, and its circulation, our entire physical system would collapse. In essence, the practice of Tai Chi helps us to recover our own inherent powers of self-healing. Contemplation on this actuality acts to protect and balance our "vital energy"(*chi*).

Through the cultivation of *chi*, the student will have a splendid opportunity to better regulate the physiological wonderworkings of the human organism.

The dynamic force of *chi* is not restricted to the human body and we need to look at the evidentiary data that identifies this subtle energy.

As a case in point, Western science is aware of electrical fields of energy which exist within the earth's atmosphere. The 'Van Allen Belt' is one such example, as well, there exist other fields of electromagnetic energies found resting in mountains, beaches, parks and open spaces which are strongly charged and carry regenerative energy in the form of 'negative ions.'

This negative ionization, which traditional Chinese medicine has been familiar with for over four thousand years, is sub-classified as *'kong-chi'* (goong chee).

Negative ions form an essential part of the eco-system and are nurturing elements needed for human growth and physiological homeostasis. Within the human organism, on the sub-molecular level, these ions are instinctively directed toward sustaining overall health in much the same way that vitamins and minerals supply nutrition for the body.

It appears that the lining of the nasal passages and sinuses are especially sensitive to the negative ions in the atmosphere. Subsequently we can see that slow, deep, and rhythmic breathing, filtered exclusively through the nasal passages, is a primary key in absorbing and regulating the energy of *chi!*

When it comes to detecting and extracting the bionic energy carried in the air, the nose knows best!

In Tai Chi, the earth is seen as a reservoir of energy for *chi*, which aside from the organ of the nose, is absorbed by the body through a specific route that starts through the feet and continues up through the legs, carries along the spine, extends through the arms and finally arrives at the hands and fingers.

Correct **grounding**, or if you will, proper 'earth-contact,' stabilizes and energizes the divergent electrical fields of the body. In Tai Chi, the torso and back are in a relaxed and 'upright' position; with the back held naturally straight the *chi* will flow along the spine and reach the brain more efficiently.

In practice, there is a deliberate slowing of physical motion, and when coupled with measured respiration, neuro-electric force is effectively harnessed. The controlled actions and maneuvers, related to the 'dance of movements,' further instigates increased circulation which more efficiently conducts nutrients and oxygen to varied tissues and organic structures.

Setting aside the nitrogen/oxygen atmosphere which engages the human organism to thrive, within the air we breathe is another form of vital energy, which in Chinese medical terminology, as mentioned earlier, is distinguished as **kong-chi.**

In Tai Chi, we refer to the nutrient value of air, as **kong-chi** and our *chi* is conveyed throughout the human body via an independent and parallel configuration analogous to the nervous system and which also happens to help regulate electrical force.

Once again, deeper rhythmic breathing supplies the body with much needed fuel taken in as kong-chi which may be viewed or translated as refined oxygen. This is a categorization of *chi* and its utilization is of vital importance not only for the carrying out of physical tasks, but just as importantly for the execution of mental assignments.

In essence, *chi* is the fuel for the fluent distribution of bio-energetic currents and is further subdivided into a class of *chi*, referred to as "*dur-chi*". This class of energy is specifically related to neuromuscular force, just as **kong chi** relates to circulatory force.

Chi is accessed through **points of energy** (ching-lo/acupuncture) which lie at the surface of the human body and it circulates in a deeper bed of organic material communicating with the various tissues and structures within the body.

The human body is very much like a system of levers, pulleys and weights (which are equivalent to our bony structures, tendons and muscles respectively). Like any system, it needs an energy source to operate successfully.

Without reservation, the vital organs demand energy for functional purposes in the same way that the brain requires a power-source to carry on in its primary goal, so as to discharge the measured fields of electrical energy that race to the commands of our muscular predilections.

Tai Chi practice is an exercise in stimulating the electrical force of chi and through it we enhance the relationship between the brain's impulses and its messages to the mechanical operations of the body. Creating a more rhythmic breathing pattern supplies us with deeper, more luxuriant energy and is the key factor in sustaining and cultivating our vital force while engaged in the movement-dynamics of the Tai Chi form-play.

To further clarify the scope of this approach, let us consider the two forces that operate within the structure of the human body.

One force is 'mechanical' which is responsible for moving and operating our body parts. The other is 'neuromuscular,' or living force. Neuromuscular force, is the channel-way of electrical energy which animates our muscles, tendons, and ligaments.

Again, mechanical force simply moves the bony structures of the body. However, the entire body and its workings would collapse without neuromuscular force, and this conclusion is also aptly applied to the living force of chi!

Tai Chi exercise enhances the relationship between neuromuscular force and the mechanical operations of the body, by refining the flow of chi. Breathing is kept slow, rhythmic, and deep to help the body in the distribution and regulation of chi!

Practice in Tai Chi augments our ability to be in greater command of our mental and physical functions. Furthermore, it advances and refines the talent for physical coordination and succeeds in developing mental alertness.

The central lesson in Tai Chi is the development of will. In Tai Chi we are moving toward the true *conscious* control of the framework of the human body. The climb to good health begins by trusting in the long-established instinctual design of the human organism. However, improper habits related to diet, hygiene, and postural tension, interfere with this instinctive or automatic process!

Tai Chi practice forms an arch of harmony between the mechanical and living forces of the human body and creates what might be called a 'thinking body' and supports the human desire not only for a long life, but one accompanied by sound health!

After all, what is so desirable about reaching an old age if you don't have good health!

Tai Chi realigns our thinking habits and allows us to ride the inner-wave of health to our inherent and natural state of being! Those of us who keep the peace of their *inner-self* are substantially protected from nervous and organic disturbances. The application of the body and mind to a single purpose creates an inner-calm which allows us to meet our personal goals and responsibilities with greater vigor and clarity.

The quest for sterling health has become synonymous with exercise, but most exercise systems are costly, time consuming, and exhausting, making it difficult to pursue our desire for good health and well-being.

The great popularity of Tai Chi around the world is the result of its undemanding, yet highly effective exercise techniques which require no equipment, little space, and short periods of moderate and sustained creative movement.

It is not the quantity of exercise that determines health and well-being, it is the *quality* of exercise!

Well-balanced motion and economy of movement are the key elements related to the fluid dynamics of Tai Chi form-play. In effect, Tai Chi is a study of structural dynamics as it relates to postural alignment. In essence it establishes a novel way to conserve personal strength and energy.

On the other hand, fast moving or uncontrolled muscular activity will damage muscles, tendons and joint ligaments through aggravated collision. That's why the high impact aerobic work-out, which is a stressful attack on the joints and structural supports of the body has been substantially replaced by the 'low impact' approach.

Tai Chi exercise moves with a deliberate slowness which acts to effectively stimulate a large variety of muscle groups. Most importantly, the Tai Chi method stays within the safety zone of personal performance. In Tai Chi we pay attention to the length of the muscle, and the speed with which we move so that the nerve-receptors can halt or slow down the movement before any damage can take place.

The entire physical approach is artful and composed, and the slow-motion procession enlists many more muscle groups than do sudden and quick movements. This approach lends to a complete body workout in much the same way as swimming does! This is the secret behind the Tai Chi strength building qualities, which are at once highly effective, while maintaining the physical boundaries of personal safety.

The strength and coordination acquired through the superlative techniques of the Tai Chi exercise modality can be translated into a wide variety of existing sporting events which may require upper body strength, lower body anchoring and spinal stabilization. These are sports such as, swimming, golf, basketball and tennis.

Although the form-play appears curiously ineffective due to the slow pace, the learning components provide a full range of movement-dynamics that place considerable demand on muscles, tendons, ligaments and bony structures, and are designed in such a way as to maintain the fine-line of safety over potential injury.

The rehabilitative guidelines of Tai Chi are also particularly well-suited to those who may have been injured, or who may have temporarily lost the function of the shoulder, elbow, or leg region and are not satisfied with simply masking the symptoms of pain and discomfort through continued drug use.

The function of movement can be reeducated by the appropriate body-mind coordination found in the balanced therapeutic principles of Tai Chi form-play.

As a rehabilitation tool, Tai Chi is supported by ongoing medical research, and through the graceful and focused movement-dynamics, there is great improvement of impaired function. This amelioration is accompanied by a reduction in pain and by an improvement in the condition of the injured body part.

Tai Chi is a holistic body-language that proceeds along lines of least resistance, and the slow-motion methodology is of great value to the development of overall strength, balance, and gracefulness. The sequence of sensations associated with the tempered execution of the form-play allows us to become aware of the subtle signals of the interrelated workings of the body.

Through the calculated use of personal force, Tai Chi exercise pays special attention to the circulation of nervous energy, while placing emphasis on the external conditions of body control. This artful practice helps to improve the internal condition of weakened organs, so that nature may be helped in doing its work of healing.

Tai Chi practice goes to work on the physiological environment and carries our new-found energy to the devitalized tissues and impaired organs. The chi flows to the internal structures of the body, enlivening the organic systems and supplying the required force (chi) needed for the various physical and mental operations found in the patterns of living and coping with everyday reality.

The Tai Chi viewpoint on the causes of disease emphasizes the relationship between an individual's health and his or her - diet, activity level, emotional reaction, and total overall environment.

If we want to live long and healthy, then no single aspect of human life should be considered separate from another.

Food for the body and food for the mind is the central attitude of Tai Chi!

Tai Chi is certainly an intriguing way to develop strength, coordination and heightened awareness. It is an aesthetically charming approach which provides us with an internal condition most favorable to the awakening of our own natural, self-regulating and restorative powers. The doctor treats, but it is nature that heals!

This centuries-old approach in whole-person health is a self-guiding technology. At its most fundamental level Tai Chi is a synthesis of Eastern philosophy placed in a creative bed of organically composed sculptured-movements based on nature's multifarious forces. It is a way of centering our variant energies and trains its sight on kinesthetic awareness and body alignment.

Daily practice revitalizes the mind, re-energizes the body and tranquilizes emotional content.

Tai Chi can be seen as a physical extension of consciousness. Indeed, it aims at reaching the fundamental structure of the unconscious, where through specialized fields of mental control (*chi kung-Tai Chi*), the student succeeds in uniting the whole of the divergent energies of the human organism. The primary purpose of the Tai Chi methodology is found in accessing the body's internal bio-electric field of energy and then proceeds in nurturing and further refining this delitescent force called chi.

Practice leads to a growing strength, on both physical and mental levels, which accumulates and serves the interests of individual needs. As the student becomes more sensitized to the fine ordering of his body, and more familiar with the peaceful composure which accompanies Tai Chi form-play, there comes into being a concurrent influx of energy that opens the dedicated individual to the intricate and depthless state of his mind and to a new and intensified level of self-awareness.

Tai Chi is essentially an interphasing of mind and body and although its principles are rooted in antiquity it is a technology which synchronizes physical and mental energies and aptly serves the interests of health concerns today.

In this sense we are left with a sterling example of cross-cultural provision - allowing the past to serve the present! This is actualized through a parade of artfully designed movements, or 'forms' which more accurately identifies the individual exercise strategies. These prodigious exercise-techniques are expressed in dynamic bodily portraits and have been primarily gathered from the diverse library of nature's commanding expressions, seen in animal and organic forms.

With respect to the 'martial language,' the bodily combative stances have been transposed to the more challenging demand which uses the physical body as a vehicle for developing enduring physical strength, and generating a level of mind-focalization that promotes a high degree of mental acuity.

The Tai Chi student is always on the alert, always riding toward a mind/body union that will activate the vital energy of *chi* so as to intensify conscious life.

The practitioner is steadfastly engaged in a perceptual game, found in the Tai Chi form-play, which will one day lead them to a new level of personal strength characterized as self-composure and physical-harmony. This is the aesthetic and synchronous plateau of the body-mind relationship!

The evolution of the individual who practices Tai Chi can be considered one of self-ordered change, and the student moves to advanced degrees of adaptive strength which is of prime importance in an urban-world made of floating connections and imbalanced priorities. Here within the Tai Chi framework of balanced interaction, the student finds the wellspring of subtle energies which positively affects physiological and psychological development.

Through the unbounded play of activity found in the layered Tai Chi dance that flows as one force or energy upon another, there comes into being an increased capacity to respond to changing rhythms and new vibrations, which in turn enriches the student's experience on the great wonder-wheel of life.

There is a cumulative force which is generated through Tai Chi practice and one which potentiates adaptive and more fluent methods of responding to the dynamics of everyday living. There comes as well, the development of an enriched awareness resulting in the harmonious distribution of personal energy. Moving to the higher rung of sequacious performance can well be applied to a wide palate of mental and physical endeavors.

As Charles Darwin pointed out, "Intelligence is measured by the speed and ability to adapt!" This observation succinctly sums up the inspired usefulness of Tai Chi practice. The quality of Tai Chi is to move more sensitively and with greater perception towards new frontiers of human experience, whether confined to the walls of city life, or facing the oscillating realities of the boundless universe.

Tai Chi is a fulcrum which interconnects the energies of the body and mind. It helps to develop a focal strength which balances the variable bio-forces of the human body and equalizes the mutable states of consciousness. As well, the lessons found in the Tai Chi method of engagement act to compose our emotional content.

Through the practice of the Tai Chi movement-dynamics, we are supplied with a fount of positive energy which can be given back to the world around us; to a world of social enterprise, and to a planet of which we are ultimately the caretakers. We have at our disposal an advanced body-mind development technology whose effectiveness is grounded in deep philosophical and transformational rules.

These rules are in actuality 'guidelines' that can help you regenerate personal vitality, allowing underlying creative impulses to surface. Through a selective policy of practical concepts, the Tai Chi system leads the student through a series of astute and artful maneuvers, which contribute to the union of vitality and consciousness.

This method of approach will help you unleash

deeper levels of intuitive creativity and serves the distinct purpose of allowing you to transcend feelings of self-limitation. Tai Chi has the potential to liberate you from beliefs and attitudes that are incongruous with your own sense of truth.

From a bodily perspective, Tai Chi exercise-dynamics represent a 'play on form' expressed through intriguing patterns of movement. The series of techniques can be seen as mathematical demonstrations which form a series of creative ellipses, circumambulations and geometric configurations. At the same time, Tai Chi is an artful, physical display of slowed, martial, dance-like techniques, which collectively function as an internal discipline that engages the discriminative faculty of the mind.

The techniques are designed so as to re-energize the operational strength of the body, and the balanced movements are an event in self-regeneration.

It is a learning-field where we can, more courageously, place our faith in the process, allowing the product to flower by virtue of our sustained effort. Through consistent and dedicated enterprise, where we learn to gather the spectrum of physical and mental energies, we are fed by the healthful results that come from surprisingly short periods of practice.

Indeed, it is the wise student that proceeds with a sense of dedication, for it is that in Tai Chi, dedication, rather than expectation, is the quality of being that guides us to our goal.

Although the highly effective martial techniques are respected world-wide, for the most part the self-defense elements have been left on the playing field of the 'Chinese Checkerboard' of physical executions.

"Entry into the twentieth century found the Chinese embroiled in a revival of martial fitness to cast off Manchu domination and counter growing Japanese Imperialism."

That is to say, the combative elements have fallen into the shadow of the illustrious physical articulations which are more used as a method for developing mental acuity and as a conditioning strategy and wholeness-platform for organic health and vitality.

The 'iron-man' game of aggressive power has been discarded to the thunder of primeval and instinctual battles which can still be experienced, if one is so disposed, whether as a spectator, or a warrior, through the match-play of the gaming houses of Brazil, Hong Kong, Taiwan and Hawaii.

Now, in the wizened gleam of self-propriety, Tai Chi's nonresistant method of approach acts as an agency, so to speak, for carrying the mind to higher and more creative plateaus, and is instructional in the ways in which we can conserve vital energy.

The composition of specialized movements in Tai Chi are generally referred to as 'forms' and are related to the *dance*, that is the choreography that finds expression through the techniques and body-language rooted in the martial arts. The mobilizations are designed for metabolic homeostasis and for potentiating overall physiological health, while maintaining, through moderate exercise, a highly effective degree of physical conditioning.

The exercises are used essentially as a procedure in self-discipline, which in turn create an 'anchor of will,' and serve as a pathway for self-knowledge.

Through the trial and error of mental calculations and physical logistics, the Tai Chi student may hope to succeed in gathering and focusing the entirety of the divergent energies which feed the organic structures of the human body. Through this more focalized state, the applicant then learns to reissue this collected stream-of-energy, which can be applied not only toward physical prowess and development, but equally to a quality of awareness which can be extended to those areas of life which warrant special and personal attention.

In other words, the reconstituted energy derived from Tai Chi practice further serves to intensify the field of events which compose the events of daily living.

The daily round of negativistic stress is bound up in our conformity to rules and criteria that are more designed to create "order" and undermine our capacity for natural and spontaneous self-expression. Tai Chi is a departure from imitation and uniformity. It represents a figurative and literal movement toward higher levels of awareness that nurture *individual* growth and well-being. The subtle and graceful movements of the Tai Chi form-play, in league with the intensified provision of a keen and observant mind, gradually merge to form a new standard of values that can be called upon for use in daily interactions.

The form-dynamics act as a base of self-study which allow us to direct our energy toward an inner psychic balance and mental focus that will help us discover the unique quality of our individual identity.

This points to the quality of 'central awareness' which allows us to discover our self-hood, helping us to meet the challenges and responsibilities of our personal world with amplified strength and greater clarity.

In this sense, Tai Chi is a transliteration of the whole person; not only a translation of the body, its postures and movements, but also an emotional and psychological shift toward greater self-composure.

The practice of Tai Chi leads to a new dimensional framework; a journey inward wherein the mind is suffused with a powerful flow of psychic energy.

Your sense of being will become illuminated and your state of awareness intensified in a manner that will help you to reach a life filled with greater personal meaning.

Tai Chi is an event in self-regeneration and is a vehicle which induces a transformative process where we can begin to nurture a strength seen through the development of the enduring elements of self-healing and self-composure. Through the eloquent exercises, which act upon body and mind simultaneously, we experience an integration of those energies which enliven our mental and emotional faculties. The subtle lessons of Tai Chi, seen in the rich demonstrations of 'physical portraiture,' lead to a transmogrification in self-understanding and profoundly instill a new-found positivity that can be shared with the world around us.

The evolution of the individual who practices Tai Chi can be considered an ascent toward self-healing and self-authority. Just as a fingerprint has its own unique conformation, so there exists an innate self-signature which is unmatched and original, belonging to the individual. To discover this unique, lifeblood quality, is one of the primary goals of the Tai Chi method.

Through the calculated rhythms and flowing maneuvers of the Tai Chi form-play we expand our sense of **inner time**; precious time that allows us to collect our scattered thoughts and replenish our energy. In a creative sense, we are in the throws of shaping our own universe, so to speak, and the act of generating a new world of self-order connects us more wisely to our body and mind. In the placid realm of creative enterprise we have an opportunity to recover from the hyperactivity that often undermines our capacity for emotional and mental equanimity.

Tai Chi moves from a creative platform designed for bodily articulations, which require focused attention on a set of physical maneuvers, and covers a spectrum of techniques that realign the physiological and organic structures of the human body.

This is the challenge that Tai Chi offers; developing creative physical skills and coordination, enhancing mental focus, and generating a more complete self-awareness. When this "balance" is experienced, profound positive effects are felt reaching the most sensitive side of human nature, and that is to say - *emotion.*

Indeed, Tai Chi retrains the psyche and reconstitutes our physical energy, generating a course of action that strips away the accumulated layers of impersonality and in so doing creates a higher vehicle for the uniqueness of human sensitivity and expression.

The positivity of creative, personal growth and its unequivocal effects on emotional well-being is the character of Tai Chi.

In its essential form, Tai Chi expresses a mystical feeling of being one with yourself and yet not separate from the world around you. This ancient art passes humbly across the cultural bridge of Western sensibilities and teaches us to accept our humanity. It further discloses a method of approach that supports the quality of the human spirit and embraces the magnificent mechanisms of the human body. The integration of physical, mental and emotional states is at the heart of the Tai Chi philosophy.

Tai Chi is not a passive obsession with inner-directed contemplation, but is a selective pursuit that matures in outwardly involved social operations. Can we not see that social action is the theater of affairs that tests the validity of our 'interior clarity' and self-order?

Regretfully, the Western mind gravitates toward certain singular themes of oriental substance and has a lop-sided view of Tai Chi's traditional approach as a whole.

A new light is needed as we reach ever closer to the shores of what is becoming a global community, and in our philosophical evolution the time has come to see beyond mere platitudes and past the distorted viewpoints that paralyze our sense of humanity.

The moment that is upon us points to a greater appreciation of the challenging and more profound philosophical elements related to Tai Chi's authentic approach to inspired health and human conduct.

The Enchanted Machine

*"The future weighs less
than the past - and dreams
weigh less than experience."*

— E. Starjava

The pioneers of physical training and health-related exercise have blazed a trail for the common man and woman, and we are all, more and more, recognizing the importance of cultivating enduring physical strength and applying our time and energy toward developing greater mental acuity.

In the past decade a new training-system in health-care and personal development has surfaced. Although this method of approach was expressly constructed in the thirteenth century, the principles of Tai Chi exercise actually span a plurality of generations, and can be traced historically to the founder of Chinese surgery, namely physician Hua T'ow (d. 2), who devised a system of exercise techniques based on a variety of animal posturings derived from their fighting habits in dealing with survival.

Hua T'ow's fighting system was called the 'Five Animal Forms,' and included specialized breathing exercises (chi-kung) already well known to the medical field for some two thousand years. The initial dimensions of this ancient combat system evolved into the multi-disciplinary approach named 'Tai Chi Ch'uan,' pronounced 'tie jee chew-en.' The contemporary translation of Tai Chi (ch'uan) is commonly viewed as "the grand/ultimate," which is a rather grandiose interpretation that poorly serves its modest attitude. Perhaps we can venture to propose that Tai Chi may also be considered to mean; "distinguished/celebrated," which is more in keeping with its unassuming character.

The title just mentioned is attached to the operative term, namely: "ch'uan" meaning 'fist,' and once again we are confronted with a paradoxical issue that suggests 'combat,' when in actuality, and to the dismay of many teachers, the pugilistic elements have considerably receded in recent decades.

What might be more appropriate when defining this antique title is a philosophical viewpoint that is married to the idea of an **encounter** with 'the sublime and eminent way.' However it may be, 'Tai Chi' has become a shorthand term for a growing movement that is reshaping the fabric of preventative health-care, and in an unassuming manner is painting its strength of character on the phenomenology of exercise.

Tai Chi is a direct outgrowth of traditional Chinese medicine and is prescribed for such debilitating conditions as coronary heart disease, high blood pressure, and respiratory ailments, including pulmonary tuberculosis and asthma.

Empirical studies support its efficacy in regulating metabolism and improving blood circulation, and further point to the salubrious effects on minimizing mental stress and treating psychological neurosis. Tai Chi has proven its efficacy in dealing with these and a wide range of medical pathologies, which we will shortly cover while examining the full health benefits in terms of a medical assessment.

Perhaps what is most intriguing about Tai Chi is that it has developed an aesthetic interplay of techniques that captures a powerful component underlying the complexity of form and movement. It has shown us a way to access the storehouse of life-energy that plays directly into the quality of our mental and physical well-being.

Tai Chi has spawned its own language; an organic and elegant jargon of "Crane Fans Wings;" "Parting the Wild Horse's Mane;" "Wave Hands Like Clouds," and other characterizing terms that represent novel elements of motion.

These 'word-portraits', so to speak, serve as choreographic reminders for the exercise regimen which may be composed of up to one hundred and twenty-four separate techniques. Tai Chi has been popularized through an exercise series known as the "Twenty-Four (movements) Short-Form," which is an abbreviated framework that has been rigorously tested by medical standards. The physical elaborations dramatically improve structural alignment and foster mental acuity through shaping the body and mind through a series of movements that are caught up in the phraseology taken ultimately from Nature's grand display of living forces. This eminent health-care approach integrates martial art posturings, special breathing regulation (*chi kung*), and engages the subtle aspects of the 'focalizing' components of meditation.

Tai Chi is based on an eclectic body of knowledge taken from Taoist and Buddhist principles of energy-conservation and their health-care methods. Tai Chi addresses the search for longevity and the quest for self-authority as it proceeds to create the ultimate defense against a formidable enemy that we can't see - *stress!*

The ancient Chinese recognized this 'unseen' enemy, and for literally thousands of years neutralized the stress-response by the practice of natural and organically based exercises.

The therapeutic value of China's preeminent exercise modality known to you as Tai Chi has been scrutinized since 1950 by the foremost *Chinese National Sports Committee.* The supervisory board has categorized various approaches in exercise therapy, with *chi-kung,* being a combination of breathing-therapies and mind-exercise modalities, emerging as the leading therapeutic method. *Chi kung* happens to be the nucleus of the science of Tai Chi, and during the last decade has been undergoing extensive research by Western medical and sports professionals.

The varied and distinct approaches in the *mind-body* health-field which includes biofeedback, autogenic training, deep breathing, and guided imagery, are Western extractions of the essence of *chi-kung.*

Research amongst athletic professionals has identified a strong public need for alternative exercise programs which are both effective and safe. Tai Chi is demonstrably creative in its training approach which acts to inform and educate the student in an exercise methodology that is used for the development and maintenance of qualitative physical conditioning, enhanced mental focus, and psychological equilibrium.

The general public has been, over recent years, demanding access to information in health areas formerly held exclusively by professionals. This includes information about the effects of therapy, drugs, non-surgical alternatives, nutrition, methods of preventive medicine and a whole host of related areas in health maintenance and general self-improvement.

The extremely effective work done in the Tai Chi modality follows from over four millennia of experience with traditional Chinese medicine in treating internal conditions of body and mind. Recent studies in the West show that moderate, daily exercise will promote fitness, health and a longer life. In fact, investigations show that a moderate intensity exercise-program will counter the cumulative daily impact of the stress-response while lowering blood pressure, reducing negative cholesterol levels, and improving cardiovascular fitness in the same range as high-intensity workouts.

Groups doing as little as five minutes of brisk walking, every two days, had less than half the incidence of heart disease than a sedentary group. Because of these findings, Tai Chi's popularity is increasing steadily throughout Europe, the United States and Canada, due in great part to its extensive efficacy in the treatment of a variety of health-related problems ranging from minor to more severe.

Let us now consider Tai Chi in terms of a medical assessment which has been provided to us by the China Sports Editorial Board.

These traditional exercise modalities form an important part of the treatment, often prescribed in hospitals and sanitariums. Tai Chi has proved its efficacy in treating chronic diseases such as high blood pressure, neurasthenia and pulmonary tuberculosis. Certain nervous and mental diseases are relieved of pathological excitation enabling the cerebrum and cerebral cortex an opportunity to rest.

At the same time, the high degree of concentration required in the Tai Chi exercises benefits the function of the central nervous system by causing positive excitation in certain regions of the cerebral cortex and exhibiting protective inhibition in other zones. This is accomplished through training the mind and body at the same time and stimulating the brain into the production of endorphins and encaphalons which contribute to a state of physical and mental well-being.

Regular practice of Tai Chi results in an increased supply of blood to the coronary arteries, more forceful heart contractions, and improved hemo-dynamic processes.

Moreover, Tai Chi appears to improve the regulatory functions of various organs in the human body, increase the tension of the vagus nerves, insure adequate supplies of blood and oxygen to the tissues of the various organs and helps to facilitate substance metabolism - all of which contribute to a lower incidence of hypertension and arteriosclerosis.

Constancy in the practice of Tai Chi exercises can increase the elasticity of the lung tissues, enlarge the respiratory magnitude of the chest (which helps to retard the ossification of the rib cartilage), increase the ventilatory capacity of the lungs, and improve the exchange of oxygen and carbon dioxide.

The greater, vital lung capacity results from a stronger diaphragm and the increased muscular capacity of the thoracic walls. The abdominal respiration accompanying Tai Chi exercises will help ventilation of the lungs and through rhythmic changes of abdominal pressure, speed up blood flow and gas exchange in the alveoli pulmonum.

Tai Chi exercise also strengthens bones, muscles and joints. Since many of the movements and postures hinge on the axis turning of the waist and involve a great deal of lumbar movement, systematic exercise can be helpful to the form and structure of the lumbar vertebrae, and indeed the spinal column as a whole.

Along with greater flexibility of the spine, bones receive a greater supply of blood and this may help to significantly reduce or eliminate senile osteoporosis.

This degenerative affliction may be caused by such factors as reduced blood supply to the bones owing to arteriosclerosis. There is also the factor of poor absorption of calcium and potassium present in food due to the lack of hydrochloric acid in the gastric juices.

Insofar as Tai Chi can prevent or lessen such disorders, its role in retarding the aging process is noteworthy.

In recent years, researchers have studied the role of physical exercise in delaying senescence and Tai Chi's temperate approach is significant in the province of longevity.

Aging is associated with poor circulation due to the hardening of the arteries, and cholesterol which plays directly into the condition of the artery walls drops substantially for those engaged in regular Tai Chi exercise.

Some experiments conducted on elderly people afflicted with arteriosclerosis reveal that after five or six months of Tai Chi training, there is an increase of albumin and a marked decrease of globulin and cholesterol in the blood specimens taken.

Through regular practice the whole body develops in balance due to the nature of the artful exercises which render one's thinking lucid and one's mind peaceful, steadily increasing the individual's vital force and physical energy.

The Bridge of Human Wisdom

"Sometimes the best teacher is one
who instructs a single child
or enlightens a grownup
who is past hope."

— anon

The first martial scientists who set the discipline of Tai Chi into motion had an eye for pattern, especially when concerned with aesthetic symmetry and natural order. They had a taste for complexity, for circular rather than linear approaches, and were fascinated with mindful, geometric journeys that led to personal balance and self-revelation.

They speculated about the nature of conscious intelligence and the process of change. They observed the many and were looking for the whole.

For those who fell upon the way of Tai Chi, they perceived it to be a dance of self-illumination; a treading that transported the soul to the summit of man's intelligence and beyond to the gate of human compassion.

They held true to an ancient legacy and through its artful excursion into the present, we are inspired with a gentle whirl of consciousness to discover the body and mind flowing with fluid order and symmetry. In this pristine state we awaken to the real journey of life. We are given over to the sequence of Tai Chi's resplendent form-play and festive movement-dynamics which offer us a definition for creative enterprise and personal truth.

The core of Tai Chi is found in emotional and mental conservation; temperate, graceful, and flowing with subtle drama, there is more to the appearance of Tai Chi than meets the naked eye. What seems to be soft is a disguise for internal strength, and what appears to be slow, is a mask for creative intensity. The flow of Tai Chi moves with the forces of nature - ever-changing, yet ever constant.

As we practice this ancient body-mind art-form, there is the sense of an endless liquescent excursion which explodes into smaller exquisite journeys of pure awareness. Then we find ourselves in some spaceless, timeless dimension where we are left holding our hearts as we would embrace a newborn child. It is a place inside ourselves where we are left holding our minds as we would light upon a butterfly.

Gentle and strong, creatively peaceful, we experience the gracefulness of the open soul and we find ourselves exposed to the sacred bareness of the unbounded spirit. The mind reaches toward the vault of heaven and with our feet against the bosom of the earth we feel whole again. We step on the clouds of imagination and are transported to that secret space within us, to some far away place in motionless time where there is the sense that we may have forgotten who we once were, but are clear about who we can still become.

Outer individual/inner self; spirit/personality; child/adult; whoever you are, within you lives the life of the universe, and within your hands you hold the key to your purpose.

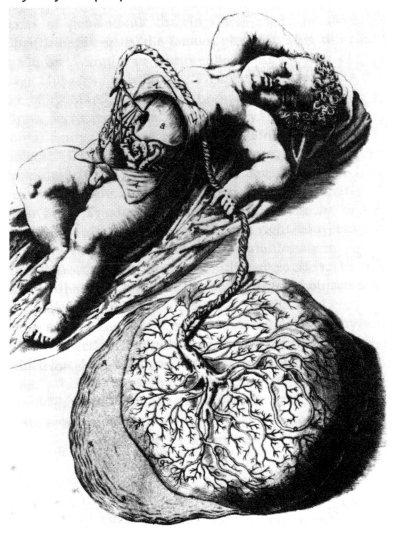

"Within you lives the ageless child and the life of the Universe."

You have been gifted with the Tao!

In your heart are great wings that have taken your imagination and curiosity into the mysteries of dreams, and you have always hoped to convert your visions into a reality for the greater well-being of your life and those dear to you.

Within the vortex of our emotional content we may discover the ageless child, and if we are patient, within the child will grow a flower, forever extending toward the canopy of stars; eternally in search of the celestial waters of self-reality.

Through the organic procession of movements, which take flight in the great dance of Tai Chi, we move to a deeper level of awareness and come face to face with the origin of the vital force which sustains our lives. The rhythm of the universe manifests its primeval force through the endless forms of human evolution.

Like a river, the current may change, but will inevitably lead us to an internal awakening. It is an awakening which releases us from the narrow limits of uniformity and imitation, and liberates us from the marginal experiences as endured by the heart. Awareness is freed from the powers of dissolution found in our ego-based responses.

To study Tai Chi is to study yourself!

Not only are you presented with your potential, but with your limitations as well. And what is most important is to learn how to accept both - gracefully!

Many of our limitations are in fact obstacles on the path to greater self-discovery. In the practice of Tai Chi, as in life, we are presented at various times with an impasse, a barrier in our development. The attitude in Tai Chi, is learning to accept this as proof of how far we have progressed; how far we have come to be faced with yet another challenge and to have the opportunity to find out who we are in the unfolding of a new process - in a new adventure.

Remember, that self-confidence is gained as we repeatedly overcome doubt!

If you concentrate on what you can do now, in the moment of your effort, then you will cultivate a new-found freedom and simplicity wherein your internal strength will surface.

Tai Chi has long been called the dance of meditation, but it is also a method of self-cultivation which enriches the fertile fields of the mind, providing those who are dedicated with focused awareness and inner strength, so as to deal more effectively with this world of scattered energies, unstable circumstances, and unexpected changes.

The practice of Tai Chi leads to a new self-image based not on our propensity to dominate and appropriate, but rests more gracefully on our capacity for self-composure and self-regeneration. With each step we are taught to move beyond our mechanistic patterns, and within its gentle circle of simplicity we are inspired to move toward genuine self-civilization.

From technique and strength of body in the beginning, to a profound realization of self in the end - that is the journey of Tai Chi!

Once again, in the history of Man's wondrous and precarious ascent, we find ourselves at the crossroads of an internal revolution with science and technology forcing us into new stances and offering new possibilities, presenting us with yet another set of criteria which topples the patterns we have not even gotten used to. Those of us who see beyond the technical glitter, are charged to continue our search for other avenues of experience which will give us a

"*From technique and strength of body in the beginning, to a profound realization of self in the end - that is the journey of Tai Chi.*"

sense of truth and a deeper meaning for living. It is *we*, after all, who are at the center of this expanding universe.

Indeed, human beings have come to rule this sacred planet, and if we are to safeguard this precious *sphere*, it cannot be achieved by a wholly materialistic attitude, nor a wholly spiritual one!

There is a third conceptual framework which acts to unite the two. It is not a mixture, not a 'half and half,' but an expanded structure of reference that will help us come to realize that the spiritual aspect of our being and that which is physical and material are interdependent.

In other words, consciousness and action must act as one!

If we are to drink from the cup of wisdom, then we must be patient with ourselves and our development; and we must also reach more deeply into our emotional content, so as to counterbalance the perennial activities of the intellective mind and allow the *essential self* to shape the events of our life-pattern.

We have arrived at the gateway of the great revolution in understanding the human body, and perhaps one day we will comprehend the full workings of the human mind.

This ancient map in self-healing, which goes by the name of Tai Chi, offers a profound, yet uncomplicated approach for seeing the pieces of man's life fall, ever more gently, into the puzzle of self-reality.

If a picture paints a thousand words, then let us paint a new canvas for personal experience; as the Chinese say, let us *play* Tai Chi and continue our search for the secret palace of longevity and for the hidden jewel of human intuition. To do so, we need to prepare the physical body so as to understand the human mind - and let us understand the mind to see the self! When the wondrous instrument of mind joins in harmony with the enchanted vehicle of the body, then will the windows of perception be clear to see the infinite landscape of self-reality- revealed is the priceless value of egoless, naked existence.

"There is a calling-vision for a peaceful stopping at the bridge of human wisdom."

In the great circle of endless time, human life is but a single breath.

In a universe of countless forms, man appears as a grain of sand. Yet to each of us, we see this breath as infinitely long and precious, and this grain of sand, as a world that cannot be fully traversed.

To fathom the reality of mind is the great conundrum - the formidable knot that we must ultimately untie. To draw away the curtain of illusion and scale the barrier of self-doubt is the great work!

How long will humankind remain sitting in the halls of learning, imitating the deeds and words of the ancients?

We may hope to arrive at breadth of knowledge, but still remain ignorant. We may come to understand the value of great effort, but still remain ineffective.

When will man's learning become wisdom? When will his knowledge bring peace to the world? How will he arrive at this wondrous scene where the waves will be stilled and the wind calmed?

Deep in the rushing, spawning seas of Man's awareness, some few will perceive that life is not a problem to be solved, but a reality to be experienced. Hopefully, there will come a history that sees man untying the "Gordian knot" of self-obscurity.

In some other, higher orbit of awareness, divine maturity will eventually enter man's life-pulse and send him plunging into the subtle wonder of stillness and peace.

We will find ourselves stepping beyond the narrow confusion of private opinion and with new inspiration humankind will more gracefully transcend the *obsession* with contrived activity.

Yes, somewhere ahead, beyond the thin white cities, beyond the dramatic inertia of material preoccupation, the mountains ring with primal calls of self-reality, as the fleeting shadows of great and wondrous wings race across the stone-palace hills, reminding us of our quest for a freeing openness.

There is a calling-vision for stillness, compassion and preservation, and for a peaceful stopping at the bridge of human wisdom.

May good fortune and loving favor shine upon your journey through life!

And until we meet again

    ... Keep the faith

      ... Increase the peace

        ... Lead from the heart

          ... And always be yourself!

For an in-depth exploration of the principles and movement-dynamics of the Tai Chi exercise-system you can accompany Master Instructor Joey Bond on the nationally syndicated PBS television series entitled:

"Tai Chi INNERWAVE"

Discover for yourself Tai Chi's ancient dance of movements available on a 3 hour instructional video, and a CD of original music accompanied by a scholarly booklet on the "I Ching;" all offered through:

ProMotion Publishing
3368-F Governor Drive, Suite 144
San Diego, Ca. 92122
1-800-231-1776

As well as the local PBS Television Station in your vicinity or you may call:

1-800-TAI-5595